MW00453479

DILOGGÚN TALES
—— OF THE ——
NATURAL WORLD

"Ócha'ni Lele's *Diloggún Tales of the Natural World* is a historic glimpse into the beauty and power of the Lukumi religion. Readers will not only find this book educational and inspirational but deeply transformative."

IFALADE TA'SHIA ASANTI,
SENIOR BOOK REVIEWER AT *URBAN SPECTRUM* NEWSPAPER

"Ócha'ni Lele gives both the initiated and the layperson a true sense of the marvel and mystery within the pataki, the sacred stories of Afro-Cuban Santería. As with previous works, reading *Diloggún Tales of the Natural World* is like sitting at the feet of an elder while dramatic stories filled with vibrant characters are woven together to reveal universal truths of human existence. These stories, committed to the page, are an invaluable gift to those of us living long distances from our godparents and spiritual homes. Ócha'ni Lele is turning a vast and rich oral tradition—one book at a time—into an eloquently written one. We give thanks to the orisha themselves for choosing him as their messenger."

IRETE LAZO,
AUTHOR OF *THE ACCIDENTAL SANTERIA*

"At the heart of Ifa, Lukumi, Santería, and various other Yoruba-influenced traditions in the African diaspora is the diloggún, the complex cowrie-divination ritual by which devotees ascertain the will of the orishas. At the heart of the diloggún are the patakís, stories that elaborate upon and explain the various figures formed by the falling shells. Ócha'ni Lele has put much of this oral tradition in print, offering us an invaluable view into the complexity and beauty of Yoruba mythology and culture. Like most fairy tales, these legends are simple but carry deep and profound truths: *Diloggún Tales of the Natural World* is a book that has something to offer adherents, scholars, and curious neophytes alike."

KENAZ FILAN,
AUTHOR OF *THE NEW ORLEANS VOODOO HANDBOOK* AND
THE HAITIAN VODOU HANDBOOK

"*Diloggún Tales of the Natural World* is essential reading for anyone interested in the myths and superstitions of Cuba and the Caribbean. This book is entertaining and extremely informative, especially when explaining the role religion played during and after the African slave trade."

XAVIANT HAZE,
AUTHOR OF *THE SUPPRESSED HISTORY OF AMERICA*

DILOGGÚN TALES
— OF THE —
NATURAL WORLD

*How the Moon Fooled the Sun
and Other Santería Stories*

ÓCHA'NI LELE

Destiny Books
Rochester, Vermont • Toronto, Canada

Destiny Books
One Park Street
Rochester, Vermont 05767
www.DestinyBooks.com

Destiny Books is a division of Inner Traditions International

Copyright © 2011 by B. Stuart Myers

All rights reserved. No part of this book may be reproduced or utilized in
any form or by any means, electronic or mechanical, including photocopying,
recording, or by any information storage and retrieval system, without permission
in writing from the publisher.

Library of Congress Cataloging-in-Publication Data
Lele, Ócha'ni, 1966–
  Diloggún tales of the natural world : how the Moon fooled the Sun, and other
Santería stories / Ócha'ni Lele.
    p. cm.
  Includes bibliographical references and index.
  ISBN 978-1-59477-419-5 (pbk.) — ISBN 978-1-59477-803-2 (e-book)
  1. Santeria. 2. Mythology, Cuban. 3. Nature—Mythology. I. Title.
  BL2532.S3L45 2011
  299.6'7413—dc23

                                                              2011023534

Printed and bound in the United States

10   9   8   7   6   5

Text design by Priscilla H. Baker
Text layout by Virginia Scott Bowman
This book was typeset in Garamond Premier Pro with Greymantle, Rage Italic,
and Trajan Pro used as display typefaces

To send correspondence to the author of this book, mail a first-class letter to the
author c/o Inner Traditions • Bear & Company, One Park Street, Rochester, VT
05767, and we will forward the communication.

For my muse, Ivelisse Pesante. Ivy, you came into my life at just the right time, a point when I was about to put my pen down forever. Thank you for both your friendship and your inspiration.
May Oshún keep you in her arms forever!

CONTENTS

PREFACE

As of this writing, a year has passed since I published my first volume of short stories titled *Teachings of the Santería Gods*.* It was a collection of tales based on the oral narratives of the Lucumí faith, religious stories known to practitioners as patakís. Many of these chronicles existed only as oral fragments although a few were written in barebones fashion in the *libretas* (spiritual notebooks) kept by priests and priestesses. I brought them together in a coherent form, gently nurturing them through the transformation from oral tales to written literature. All were an extension of my studies as a diviner with the diloggún, which itself is both an oral holy book and a system of divination. My reasoning for this project was simple—the stories themselves are worthy of study by not only the priesthood and laity, but also by those attempting to understand our spiritual practices. In the preface to *Teachings of the Santería Gods* I wrote:

> . . . these stories [the patakís] are legends comparable to those found in the ancient myths of Greece and Rome; they are as culturally significant as those in the Torah, Talmud, or Christian Bible; they are rich with jewels of wisdom like the I Ch'ing, and they are as vast as the

---

*Ócha'ni Lele. *Teachings of the Santería Gods* (Rochester, Vt.: Destiny Books, 2010).

Vedas of the Hindu faith. There are stories about the creation of the world, the birth of Olódumare (God), and the resulting Irunmole (the first orishas) who awakened in heaven; there are myths describing the lives of the holy odu themselves as they walked on Earth in mortal form. There are histories about ancient priests, and kings, and commoners—people who lived and died following the ways of the orishas. Finally, there are stories about the orishas themselves—the loves, losses, conquests, and defeats making them the powerful beings they are today. There are mantras and songs, hymns and chants, ritual customs and secular teachings: one finds all this, and more, in the patakís of the odu.*

Teachings of the Santería Gods began as an extensive project in 2002 after penning the manuscript for *The Diloggún: The Orishas, Proverbs, Sacrifices, and Prohibitions of Cuban Santería.*† Having sent *The Diloggún* to the publisher, I wrote an extensive collection of rough drafts based on the Yoruba and Lucumí myths. Beginning with the root odu of the diloggún, known as Okana (represented by the number 1), moving chronologically through each family of odu, and culminating with the odu Ejila Shebora (represented by the number 12), I drafted, wrote, and rewrote more than a thousand stories in eight years. It was a lot of work, more writing than I've done in my entire life.

Still, space constraints in a single book restricted me to those stories I felt best illustrative of each odu's energy and meaning. For each story I included, as many as a hundred or more were left out. *Teachings of the Santería Gods* was an expansion of my previous volumes published through Destiny Books; however, too many stories

---

*Lele, *Teachings*, 3.

†Ócha'ni Lele, *The Diloggún: The Orishas, Proverbs, Sacrifices, and Prohibitions of Cuban Santería* (Rochester, Vt.: Destiny Books, 2003).

remained unused, tucked away in my hard disk drive where they were of little good to anyone except me. Following my sincere belief that these stories do not belong to me, that I am only their transcription-ist and caretaker, I went back through my collection and looked for themes among them beyond the unifying thread of the diloggún and its 256 sacred odu; and once I identified those themes, I began pulling them together in groups suitable for publication. In my quest to share knowledge of the divine orishas with both Lucumí adherents and the world at large, I created this volume of stories titled *Diloggún Tales of the Natural World: How the Moon Fooled the Sun and Other Santería Stories*. While all the stories come from different places in the dilog-gún spanning the sum total of the 256 odu, their unifying thread here is that of the natural world and natural phenomenon. Each is a separate study of some spiritual principle in nature—the waxing and waning of the moon, the solar and lunar eclipse, the phenomenon of shooting stars, the icy chill of the wind, and the first animals and birds who crept on the earth or flew through the skies—yet each com-bines to enrich the reader's study and knowledge of the spirituality behind the Lucumí faith and orisha worship. Far from primitive, the Yoruba were a deeply religious people with a well-thought-out system of metaphysics and theology, which guided their faith and day-to-day lives. This spirituality pervades modern culture in ways the average person might not understand, from the Cuban batá drums to Latin music to the African American tall tales and yarns. Yoruba spiritual-ity is their deepest root and embraces them all.

As with all my writings, I offer this book not as an exhaustive sur-vey of the oral literature but as an expansive work building on things I have done before. Hopefully, it provides a foundation on which other Lucumí writers can base their own work. I have opened both my note-books and my heart as I offer the fragments I have from my own stud-ies, and I pray that others with knowledge can add theirs to mine. For as I wrote in *Teachings of the Santería Gods*, the odu Unle Odí (8-7) tells us that Olódumare spread his knowledge and wisdom through creation; and if we are to evolve and grow, we must bring that wisdom back together and share.

If the spirituality of the orishas is about nothing else, it is about growth and evolution. I pray that we all evolve into something greater than our individual selves and wisdom.

ÓCHA'NI LELE
WINTER PARK, FLORIDA, 2011

ACKNOWLEDGMENTS

As a writer I've been privileged to work with the best editorial and support staff in the industry and I am indebted to each of them. My editors over the years helped me grow in ways unimaginable when I first put pen to paper: Susannah Noel, Doris Troy, Nancy Ringer, and Patty Capetola were tireless and thorough in their work with each volume published by Destiny Books, an imprint of Inner Traditions International. The staff at Inner Traditions, especially Laura Schlivek, Erica Robinson, Mindy Branstetter, and Jon Graham, were wonderful mentors as I wrote each manuscript. Finally, I am thankful that the publisher himself, Ehud Sperling, accepted each work as it came to his desk.

As a student I have been blessed with wonderful English and creative writing professors who guided me not only in classroom curriculum but also in my work as an author: Professors Ann Refoe, Terie Watkins, Webb Harris, and Virginia (Ginger) Magarine, all with Seminole State College in Sanford, Florida. While finishing the collection of stories for this volume I was a student in Professor Watkins' English II class and in Professor Magarine's Creative Writing I workshop. I would like to give Professor Magarine special thanks for honing my skills as a storyteller. She was an inspirational instructor.

I'd like to thank my spiritual godparents, Banacek "Checo Yemayá" Matos and Angel "Coquí Oshún" Jimenez: because of both of you, there are few men in this world who are as blessed as I. Every day, people write to me about the nightmares they lived in their quest for ocha; and they tell me about the traumas they go through on a daily, weekly, monthly, and yearly basis with their own godparents. Too many santeros wander the world, lost and incomplete, because once ocha is given they are abandoned, turned out into the world to fend for themselves, spiritually and otherwise. Each year that passes I feel closer to you both; I hope we stay like this forever.

I need to thank all of the "serious" godchildren in my life at this time: Ashara Yvonne Watkins, Katelan V. Foisy, Jason Jernigan, Robert Young, Rebecca Payn, Vivienne D'Avalon, Sandy Short, Kourtnie Dionne Nandlal, Stephanie Adele Simons, Kitty Mundis, Kenny Mundis, David Hess, Amy Fischetto, Ian Cook, Keith Bonner, Weikeen Loh, Joice Loh, and Ricardo Valencia. Every time I put my pen to paper, or my fingers to my keyboard, you are the ones who inspire me to continue this work. After I am gone from this world, each of you will still be around, and each of you will have your own religious godchildren. In my absence, my books will be here to instruct you, and my private notes will be in your hands to guide you. Seriously, I think about things like this—what will become of you when I'm gone? For no other reason, that's why I keep writing and putting absolutely everything I know and everything I learn on paper. The printed word, published and otherwise, will live after my death; and my spiritual descendants will have a part of me with them as they grow, spiritually. This is but a small part of my legacy to each of you—and it is for this reason, and no other, that I stay up all night, writing.

The world should thank you for inspiring me.

Finally, I would like to thank the thousands of readers who have supported my work over the years by buying and reading my books. An author without an audience is a lonely creature, and your comments, criticisms, and praises have kept my pen in motion throughout the years. Thank you!

INTRODUCTION
THE IMPORTANCE OF PATAKÍS

In the Book of Genesis, Noah cursed Ham and his descendants to spend their lives as servants and slaves. In Genesis 9:25 he told them, "Cursed be Canaan! The lowest of slaves will he be to his brothers." Twisted theology identified those with dark skin as the descendants of Ham, opening the way, theologically speaking, for both the Catholic and Protestant churches to declare Africa a storehouse of free labor for the New World. Yet just as the major sects of Christianity differed on their principles of theology, so did they differ on the principles of the treatment of slaves. Viewing them as human animals, dark-skinned humanoids whose skin bore only a minimal resemblance to the Caucasian race, they believed their souls were tainted by sin. Such was that taint that whites labeled them a species separate and distinct from the light-skinned races. This fueled their moral righteousness in the practice. It was racism at its worst, yet slavery became more than a violent form of racism; to borrow a term coined by the British psychologist Richard D. Ryder in 1973: it became a form of speciesism based on a country's morals and religious beliefs. For if they were more like animals than

1

humans, so the masters reasoned, they deserved treatment no better than animals; and just as agricultural animals are treated differently from companion animals, so did the treatment of slaves vary, depending on the theological climate of the country in which they were enslaved.

On the shores of North America this speciesism was severe. Masters broke up and destroyed both familial and cultural ties. Each individual became a nameless, faceless unit of flesh surrounded by strangers. It was depersonalization at its worst. Each individual ethnic group represented in North America found itself confronted with other Africans having no common language; and the forced separation of those individuals fostered the loss of interpersonal communication. This was the first step toward subservience to their masters. Of this process, American scholar Henry Louis Gates wrote:

> The encounter between African languages (Yoruba, Igbo, Twi, Kikongo, and many others) and Western languages (French, Spanish, Dutch, Portuguese, English) was perhaps the most subtle and most complex aspect of the cultural confrontation that the African slaves faced in the New World. Radically abstracted from the cultural communities, and broadly dispersed from plantation to plantation, state to state, and country to country, the African slaves in much of North America soon lost the capacity to speak their own languages. Eager to "domesticate" the African slave by denying him and her those languages, their religion, their values and belief systems, and indeed their sense of order, the slave owners, first, forbade the use of African languages on their plantations. Soon after, the drum—through which those Africans speaking tonal languages (such as Yoruba) could communicate—was also prohibited. To facilitate the nefarious process of domestication, Africans from similar cultural regions were dispersed throughout various plan-

tations, in an attempt to make communication in a language other than English virtually impossible.*

But on North American shores something wonderful happened as slaves mastered a working knowledge of the English language; they shared their tribal stories with each other, and successive generations melted those stories, one into the next, until an oral literature distinctly African and fully syncretic emerged on American shores. From the various African tribes came an oral African American literature based on multiple spiritualities. No longer identified by their various ethnicities but as a single race, the "African Americans nurtured a private but collective oral culture, one they could not 'write down,' but one they created, crafted, shared with each other, and preserved for subsequent generations out loud, but outside the hearing of the white people who enslaved them, and, later, discriminated against them."† Unfortunately, as these oral literatures came together as a cohesive body of lore, their specific tribal origins were lost to successive generations.

A scholar of African American folklore and literature named Harold Courlander wrote, "The myths, legends, epics, tales, historical poems and countless other traditional oral literary forms of African peoples have been woven out of the substance of human experience: struggles with the land and the elements, movements and migrations, wars between kingdoms, conflicts over pastures and waterholes, and wrestlings with the mysteries of existence, life and death."‡ He insists that the scope of their tales is endless, dealing with all of life's struggles, conflicts, and joys. He says that their lore ". . . includes creation myths,

---

*Henry Louis Gates, "Introduction: Narration and Cultural Memory in the African American Tradition." *Talk that Talk: An Anthology of African American Storytelling.* (New York: Simon and Schuster, 1989), 15–19.

†Gates, *Talk that Talk,* 17.

‡Harold Courlander, *A Treasury of African Folklore: The Oral Literature, Traditions, Myths, Legends, Epics, Tales, Recollections, Wisdom, Sayings, and Humor of Africa* (New York: Marlowe and Company, 1996), 1.

myth-legends, half-legendary chronicles and historical narratives either in song or prose; tales that explain natural phenomena, tribal practices and taboos, and cultural or political institutions; stories and fables that reflect on the nature of man and his strengths and weaknesses; tales of adventure, courage, disaster, and love; epics with legendary heroes or fictitious heroes, and tales of confrontation with the supernatural and unseen forces of nature; moralizing stories and stories that define man's place and role in the universe; riddles that amuse and teach, and proverbs that stress social values; and a virtually inexhaustible reservoir of animal tales, many of which, at bottom, are morality plays, while others are pure humor."* In short, there is no aspect of life that African lore, and hence African American lore, does not address through story or fable.

Unfortunately, on North American shores the origin of most of these stories is lost. Modern scholars have sought to determine the ethnic origin of each fable or tall tale; however, this is modern research. As their origins are traced, many scholars discover that a single tale might have multiple roots across the Atlantic, each yarn containing elements of different ethnic groups. Some even incorporate elements of Native American spirituality, elements that are ancient but foreign to native African beliefs. In the end, the oral African American stories—from the tales of Aunt Nancy to the bedtime stories of Uncle Remus—are considered plantation tales, and no one can be sure of their true origins.

Such is not the case when dealing with the folklore of Afro-Cuban origin; and a study of African folklore and mythology in Cuba gives us a purer grasp of each tribe's spiritual beliefs. Just as the Yoruba, Igbo, Twi, Kikongo, and many other tribes were forced through the Diaspora to North American shores, so were they forced and transplanted into Caribbean cultures. For reasons we will soon understand, instead of slave masters destroying native cultures, white Cubans created miniature societies that reinforced ethic boundaries, and while tribes who

---

*Courlander, *Treasury of African Folklore*, 3.

once existed in conflict learned to support each other, they kept their spiritual beliefs virtually intact. One can study these microcosms and know, without a doubt, the origins of their beliefs.

If one can refer to slavery as kind, the system in place in Cuba was both kinder and gentler than that of its North American counterpart. For while North American practices forbade the congregation and continuation of ethnic groups, slave practices in Cuba enforced by the Roman Catholic Church sought to preserve those familial and ethnic units. As early as 1789 Charles IV, king of Spain, wrote a document titled "The Royal Document on the Trades and Occupation of Slaves." Strictly it defined the master class' duty to the subservient race: being good Catholics, all who used slave labor were to teach their charges the one true, holy religion of the Catholic Church. While Christians believed that blacks were subhuman, Church doctrine taught that they still had souls; the masters owned their bodies but God owned that which lay within. This was to be nurtured in the name of Mother Rome. Slave labor was forbidden on the high holy days of the Church, especially the feast days of the Spanish saints. On these days blacks were to attend mass and receive communion. After long days of labor they were to recite the rosary in their homes. The royal decree issued by Charles IV promised rewards for the slaves: in return for total submission to both the masters and the Church, they would be given free time to entertain and work for themselves. This benefit was lacking under Protestant demands in North America.

Further demands were issued on the slave owners by the work of two priests: Father Juan Matienzo and Bishop Pedro Augustín Morrell de Santa Cruz. These two men held black religious education in high regard. Matienzo believed that blacks were comparable, intellectually, to children and could learn something new only by comparing it to something familiar. By using their native ethnic ties, he sought to build a bridge from the Africans' paganism to the holy Catholic Church. He encouraged both priests and laymen to allow slaves to retain some of their native customs while worshipping the white supreme God. He theorized that slow acclimation and carefully calculated abdication of superstitious practices would lead each African to salvation. Having attained salvation, in time the Africans would abandon all their superstitious practices.

Bishop Pedro Augustín crusaded for black spiritual redemption alongside Matienzo. For his work, he borrowed a custom originating in fourteenth-century Seville, Spain, an organization known as the *cofradia,* or the religious brotherhood for laymen. In Spain each cofradia was dedicated to a specific saint and headed by the priests of the local church dedicated to that same holy persona. Every week members of the cofradia met in their church; the brotherhood provided religious instruction, fellowship, and support for both lifetime Catholics and new converts. Bishop Pedro Augustín rationalized that the success of the cofradia in Spain could translate into success with the conversion of slaves; and if the slaves were truly converted to the Holy Mother Church they would be more easily controlled and more productive to Spanish society. Because most churches were built in the cities themselves, the organization of the cofradia became an urban phenomenon, licensed and overseen by the existing municipalities and parishes. Soon, each church sponsored one in the name of its patron saint.

But something unforeseen happened in these societies, which soon came to be known as *cabildos,* or ethnic clubs based on each African's unique tribal identity. Instead of learning about the new Catholic faith, the members used their time to maintain and spread their natural spirituality; and each successive generation maintained their ancestors' faith. The Yoruba were particularly adept at re-creating their society and maintaining their spiritual heritage in the microcosm offered by the cabildos. Native languages were not suppressed as they were on North American shores. Instead of forbidding the use of sacred African drums, Cuban society tolerated it. Instead of using their free time to study Catholicism, Yoruba priests and priestesses maintained their ethnic customs, giving birth to a syncretic practice known as Santería. Realize, however, that the syncretism was only a facade, a mask behind which the Yoruba and their descendants disguised the worship of the orishas.

Returning again to Courlander, who writes extensively about oral African American literature, he asserts, ". . . the oral literature of Africa reflects ideas, themes, suppositions and truths that are widely shared, at the same time that it reveals creations unique to, and particularized by, a tribe, village, or region. A tribe may be united with a mainstream of African traditions and yet have legends of its own heroes, kings, and demigods, its own conflicts and migrations, and its own unique ancient origins."* The difficulty in most of these stories is unraveling their points of origin. Because North American slaves were syncretic in their storytelling, borrowing tales and ideas from not only the slave masters' literature but also Native American tribes and other African tribes, many of the resulting stories include elements that on African shores would seem foreign to each other. When studying the patakís of Lucumí faith, no such melting of stories or ideas exists. Within the cabildos' societies, the oral literature was kept pure and intact, adapting marginally to the slaves' new environment. Finally, by studying the tall tales, yarns, and oral histories of the Yoruba, scholars have a pure vision of a specific African tribe's beliefs and how its descendants managed in the harsh New World. To paraphrase Courlander, when studying the patakís of the Lucumí faith, we are studying the "myths, legends, epics, tales, historical poems and countless other traditional oral literary forms" of the Yoruba from ancient Oyó and its outlying Yoruba tributaries.† Likewise, we understand how this noble people wrestled with the concepts of life and death. It is a unique view into a single African culture.

Yet this book is not written for the scholar or those with purely academic leanings; it is written for the reader whose soul is distinctly African, the spiritual seeker whose heart finds peace and solace in the embrace of black gods. It is written for the followers of the orishas,

---

*Courlander, *Treasury of African Folklore,* 3.
†Ibid., 1.

those who know themselves as Lucumí and embrace the principles and teachings of the ancient Yoruba race. When it comes to our folklore and our beliefs, we are blessed for we know, without a doubt, that our stories and histories come from the ancient Yoruba; we need not search for their origins. The problem with oral literature, however, remains: one only tells the stories that are known, and these are, again, told to our students and godchildren. Every person has but a small piece of the whole cloth that blankets our traditions. Perhaps it is time to move beyond the oral tradition, with each of us writing down the stories we know so we can share and grow. This volume, then, is but another strand in that great cloth. In time, with works such as these, we can reweave our fragments back into a complete whole.

Before studying the stories in this book, two questions remain to be answered: What is the diloggún of which Lucumí adherents speak? And why are the patakís so important?

The diloggún is both a system of divination for Lucumí adherents and a system of categorization for Lucumí lore. In the past eleven years I've written two volumes dealing with the diloggún as a system of divination: *The Secrets of Afro-Cuban Divination* (Destiny Books, 2000) and *The Diloggún: The Orishas, Proverbs, Sacrifices, and Prohibitions of Cuban Santería* (Destiny Books, 2003). Dealing with diloggún as a system of folkloric categorization, I've written one volume: *Teachings of the Santería Gods* (Destiny Books, 2010). Because I've revisited the concept of the diloggún so many times in my previous works, perhaps the best way to describe and define this concept again is by quoting from my previous volumes:

> The word diloggún itself may be described in two fashions. First, when speaking of diloggún, one may be referring to the cowrie shells of a particular orisha, which a Lucumí priest or priestess receives upon initiation. An orisha is composed of three material

elements: otanes (sacred stones), implements, and diloggún. The otanes form the body of the deity; they are stones upon which sacrificial offerings to the orisha are given. The implements are the metal or wooden tools sacred to the orisha, the symbols by which it does its work on the earth. The diloggún, or cowrie shells, are the most important aspect of an orisha, for within these cowrie shells resides the soul of the deity. All the spirits have eighteen shells in their diloggún, except for Elegguá who has twenty-one shells, because twenty-one is his sacred number and is shared with no other spirit.*

While this passage describes the physical form of the diloggún, which are the cowrie shells received with each orisha, when divining there is a process for accessing this vast system. In *Secrets* I wrote, "The second way of defining diloggún is within the context of divination. When reading or casting the oracle, only sixteen shells from each orisha's hand of shells are used. These are picked at random, and the remaining cowries are set to the side facedown. Cowries put to the side are known as *adele* (witnesses), and while they must be present for the divination, they remain unused."† The process that a diviner uses to access this information for divination is long and drawn-out, and the best description of it can be found in chapter one of *The Diloggún*. Yet there is a complex spirituality behind this system, one that takes it beyond the realm of divination and into the sometimes-obscure world of metaphysics and African spirituality. Again, in *Secrets* I wrote:

> Unlike tools that draw on a diviner's psychic skills or subconscious mind, the diloggún is a complex system based on the sixteen holy odu made manifest when Olódumare unfolded, creating all things.

---

*Lele, *Diloggún,* 12.
†Ócha'ni Lele, *The Secrets of Afro-Cuban Divination: How to Cast the Diloggún, the Oracle of the Orishas* (Rochester, Vt.: Destiny Books, 2000).

Each odu has a name and a number of open-mouth shells associated with it; these are the parent odu of the diloggún. These sixteen signs and their numerical equivalents are: Okana (one mouth), Eji Oko (two mouths), Ogundá (three mouths), Irosun (four mouths), Oché (five mouths), Obara (six mouths), Odí (seven mouths), Unle (eight mouths), Osá (nine mouths), Ofún (ten mouths), Owani (eleven mouths), Ejila Shebora (twelve mouths), Metanlá (thirteen mouths), Merinlá (fourteen mouths), Marunlá (fifteen mouths), and Merindilogún (sixteen mouths). Spiritually, each marks a different milestone in creation, specific energy currents need to bring forth manifestation from God's womb . . . For divination, each odu may be thought of as a single chapter comparable to those found in the Christian Bible; although the literature is oral in our tradition, it is no less powerful, no less meaningful, than the most eloquently written proverbs or psalms.*

And it is here that we arrive at the diloggún's main importance to Lucumí adherents, for while divination is a practical application of this knowledge for practitioners, at its heart the diloggún is a library of oral literature, a series of books containing the sum total of Yoruba spiritual knowledge. Therefore, as a third definition of diloggún, I would like to add that at its core it is, simply, a holy book, oral though it may be. Since the earliest Yoruba sought to make sense of the world around them, they created sacred stories and proverbs that brought sense to the seeming chaos; and as the centuries progressed, they added these stories to one of the many chapters found in the odu of the diloggún. Sacred lore, magic, ebó, sacrifices, proverbs, myths, histories—all this became a part of the system. From the composite signs of Okana through the final letters of Merindilogún, they used the 256 patterns as mnemonic devices to remember the ancient stories, and they used this same system when

---

*Lele, *Secrets,* 10–11.

passing the lore from priest to priest, or within the confines of their own families. Of all religions in the world, its complexity surpasses even the Vedas of the Hindu faith.

As I present the stories in this book, a reader unfamiliar with the Lucumí faith will be exposed to many names and concepts foreign to the Western world. Of these concepts, perhaps the most unfamiliar will be those of ebó and sacrifice. Of the two, the most readily understood might be the concept of ebó, especially for those familiar with mystical Buddhist and Hindu teachings. At its core, ebó is simply an offering to a spirit or deity. There are daily rituals performed by both the Lucumí laity and the priesthood, which are similar, in many ways, to the Buddhist water ceremonies offered to their deities and ancestors. This is ebó, at least in the Lucumí mindset. Sometimes the orishas want or demand more complicated offerings, such as tobacco, rum, flowers, candles, cloths, candies, cooked foods, beadwork, or prayers. This, too, is ebó. The worship of the divinities often takes material form; and the types of ebós offered depend not only on the worshipped orisha's attributes and nature, but also on the experience of divination.

The concept of sacrifice is a bit more shocking to the sanitized Western world. There are very few native African religions that do not practice animal sacrifice; and, surprisingly, there are very few modern Western religions that do not come from a past in which sacrifice was practiced. Modern Christianity sprang from the bosom of Judaism, which at one time relied on animal sacrifice for both cleansing and the pardon of sins; and let us not forget that if the temple in Jerusalem is ever rebuilt, there are sects of Judaism that will bring back the ancient practice. Even within modern Hinduism are sects who still practice some form of sacrifice to their gods, even though most Hindus are set against the practice and advocate a vegetarian lifestyle.

Basically, the concept of sacrifice is one that believes "life feeds on life." Nothing in this world exists in a vacuum; eventually, everything is food for something else. Animals feed on plants;

animals feed on animals, and humans, as omnivores (as are some animals) feed on both. Even upon our eventual demise, creatures of the earth will feed on our bodies, and the cycle continues eternally. There is no escaping it. The concept of animal sacrifice, however, adds a spiritual dimension to the food that we eat. Much like the ritual of Jewish koshering, the animal's life is taken reverently and ceremonially, and the blood, which is the vehicle for life, nourishes the physical forms of the orishas on earth as much as the meat nourishes our own. Only God and his emissaries, the orishas, are allowed to feed on sentient life; and humans, as obscured images of the divine, are allowed to feed on the resulting death, the meat, as long as it is, for lack of a better word, hallowed. Far from being a barbaric practice, in the hands of priests and priestesses who understand the ritual's power and meaning, sacrifice becomes something beautiful and lifts our meat-eating nature beyond something primitive and into the realm of something spiritual.

Beyond these two concepts, the student of the patakís, whether a Lucumí adherent or casually interested reader, will discover that the worldview of the Yoruba, while exotic, is not that far removed from the modern world. Morals and ethics, the concept of good character and bad character, the belief in a material world driven by the spiritual realm, and a concept of karma and divine retribution (although the Yoruba never labeled it as such)—all these things are found in the ancient patakís. What will seem new is that those ancient people, a race that was maligned and forced into slavery based on Christian heresies and the evil notion that an entire continent was of the race of Ham, had such deeply ingrained spiritual beliefs and an evolved system of storytelling to back up those beliefs. All that separates this spiritual world from the mundane is the color of our skin. One will discover that within both the Africans' blackness and the Caucasians' whiteness hides a soul that is beyond color; indeed, it is beyond this world. In spite of the evils inflicted upon the Yoruba, they never lost sight of their God or their orishas. It is time to move beyond what lies without and look at what lies within; and the soulful yearnings found in these patakís might teach us that, at the end of it all, we are truly the same. We are not flesh; we are spirit, and that has no color.

1
PATAKÍS FROM
THE COMPOSITES
OF OKANA

The Separation of Heaven and Earth
From the Odu Okana Meji (1-1)

> *Death is but a journey into life*
> *and life a journey into death—*
> *but this was not always so.*

Standing between the spiritual and the material worlds is a gate known as death; we die in heaven to be reborn on earth, and we die on earth to return to heaven. The gate is thin, tenuous, yet crossing it is fatal to material beings.

As with most things in our world, it was not always like this.

There was a time when the gates between the worlds were open wide, and we crossed as easily as passing from room to room in our own homes. When the earth was new and the first generation walked on her face, no great chasm divided heaven and earth.

The first creations lived in both worlds freely, and the path between the two was unguarded. Heaven was home and the earth was the market-place, and those with time to travel could walk between the two freely.

Of course only humans and orishas had this privilege. Animals and plants were stuck in one realm or the other; and between the two, for them, was the gate known as life and death. Animals and plants, how-ever, had one power that humans did not—the power of procreation. Before dying they reproduced, and this replenished their numbers on the earth. It was for this reason, the fact that they created life from their own forms, that they could not cross the great divide—creatures born of the spiritual world were perfect, and creatures born of the mate-rial realm were less so.

In time two people noticed this: a man and a woman. They thought, "How powerful are the plants and animals—they can create life from their bodies and we cannot." They wanted to be powerful like the ani-mals so they went into heaven to petition Olófin for this ashé.

Olófin looked at them sadly, "My children—it is true that animals do re-create their own kind from their bodies, as do the plants, but have you not noticed that in the end they die? You do not die. You are eter-nal in this world."

The man spoke up first, "Yes, Olófin, we are eternal. Why would our children die like animals?"

"You are not born of earthly parents. Obatalá molded your bodies from the clay of the earth, and Olódumare gave you the breath of life. You are creatures of the perfect earth, created by Obatalá's own hands, imbued with God's very breath, the ashé of heaven. You are not bound to one world or the other."

"But I want to have a child," said the woman. Her head was bowed before Olófin, and a single tear slid from her eye. "When I see the ani-mals tending their young, I get a longing here," and she touched her womb, "and a pain here," and she folded her hands over her heart. "Surely, this is a sign?"

Olófin sighed. He was concerned, but he understood. "So be it. You will have a single child. But remember that this child is not born as you were, and as such, is not a perfect being. Instead of being molded from the sacred earth's clay by Obatalá's hands, or imbued with the breath of God, it will grow inside your belly, nourished by your own body, and when it is born it will breathe the air of this world and not the next. As such, you must never show it the gate between heaven and earth; in its earthly form, it cannot be allowed to cross as you do. It would defile and change the ashé of both worlds."

The man and woman agreed. Before the year turned the woman was with child like an animal. Neither understood the mystery, and neither knew how the child was placed in the womb. But it was there and her belly grew.

The first generation of humans marveled at the mystery of birth. They watched as the woman's belly swelled; they were afraid when her waters broke, and amid tears and pain, a new life slid from between her legs. Day by day they watched the child grow, and everyone was involved in his upbringing and education. How strange, they thought, that they were created knowing all things, but the young boy had no knowledge of anything, not even language. But learn he did. And they raised him on the stories of the orishas, and the knowledge of God and heaven, but having seen neither heaven nor an orisha the young man thought the stories to be fable and fiction.

When he was grown and able to fend for himself he told his parents, "I do not believe in the stories you raised me on. I believe in neither the orishas nor the heaven of which you speak."

His parents smiled at each other knowingly. "Son," said the mother, "You were not born as we were. Obatalá created our bodies from clay, and Olódumare himself gave us the breath of life. We know both worlds. You, however, were born from my womb. You are a child from earth and not heaven, the only one of your kind. That is why you can't cross and see heaven for yourself."

"I cannot believe in what I cannot see!" he said. "If this heaven is real, I will find it!"

The world grew dark that day; everyone tried to talk the young man out of his quest. He was unwavering. When night came and the world slept, he left the village of his birth and sought the gate between heaven and earth.

It did not take long.

He found the gate as it was in the stories of his childhood; it was beautiful and serene. He saw the path that led from this world into the next. Still he was not convinced. "I will see this heaven for myself, if it is real, and see the orishas with my own eyes." He took but a single step on the path.

Before him a great figure appeared. It was Olófin. "Child of earth!" he roared, "You were forbidden to cross this gate by your own parents. You are a creature born of earthly parents, not a human molded by Obatalá's hands and given breath by Olódumare's lips. You have defiled the ashé of this sacred place!" With those words, Olófin brought down his cane on the earth, hard; it cracked and rumbled like thunder, and the path between heaven and earth was forever broken.

That young man became an outcast that day, and the earth was forever cut off from heaven. With the gate closed, free passage was no more. As Olófin warned, the ashé of both worlds was changed when earth's only child attempted the crossing—for flesh born of flesh cannot travel into the spiritual world.

The Separation of Sky and Earth
From the Odu Okana Meji (1-1)

*It is greed that brings separation to most
things, even sky and earth.*

Just as water and land lay side by side, once Orún (the sky) and Ayé (the Earth) were only an arm's reach away from each other, with only a small space between them so animals and humans could walk. And because they were so close they were the best of friends; with nothing to do and nowhere to go, they would spend their days hunting, and whenever one of the two killed game, without thinking, he would share half his kill with the other.

Always, Orún took the head and Ayé took the lower half; it was the custom and was done without thinking.

For many centuries this is how things were.

Yet it came to pass that the earth thought itself greater than the sky; even though the sky loomed heavy and large upon her surface and she depended on the life-giving rains for sustenance, she was tired of being the one below. She sought to be the one on top.

The day came when the two hunted, and Ayé killed a jutía. In defiance she offered Orún the lower half.

"I always get the head!" said Orún.

"And I am tired of getting the butt," said Ayé.

"But I am the head; I am the crown. I am the sky, and I am the one always on top. Give me the head."

The earth defied him; she held the head tightly while holding out the lower half for her friend.

Orún gathered himself up in anger and split away from the earth. He removed himself to a place far beyond the highest mountain where earth could no longer see him.

And that was fine with her. It is for this reason that even now the sky remains beyond the reach of humans.

Yet Orún was not done with his punishment. Bit by bit, the earth's waters dried up under the sun, and as the vapors rose, Orún locked them up in his arms. He refused to let the water fall back to earth and a great drought came to the land.

The oceans receded; the rivers dried up; plants and trees withered, and all living creatures thirsted and starved.

Humans screamed at the earth, "Foolish woman—you are killing us. Make amends to the sky! Kill another jutía, and send him the head!"

Ayé was saddened by the mortal revolt; and without another thought she hunted until she killed another jutía. She removed its head and put it in the talons of a great bird. "Take this to my old friend, Orún. Tell him he has made his point. He is the head, and I will always be the world below."

That day, the bird flew into the skies and delivered the ebó to Orún. Satisfied that the earth had learned her place in the scheme of things, he released the waters he had been holding back and rain fell on earth.

The schism between heaven and earth, however, remained; and sky has never again touched the earth since the day Ayé refused to give Orún his due.

The Story of the Maja
From the Odu Okana Ejioko (1-2)

*There is none so blind as he who
refuses to see.*

For days, Maja* was exhausted. No matter how much he slept he was sleepy; and no matter how much he rested he was tired. His arms and legs ached and his skin took on a rough, sallow pallor. "Husband, you don't look well," his wife complained, worry creasing her brow.

Maja sat still, staring into space. "I feel fine, woman," he said. "I just need to rest." He put himself to bed early that evening and slept fitfully.

In the morning the sheets were sweat-soaked, and he shivered as fever warmed his flesh uncomfortably. Maja's wife put her lips to his forehead gently; it was hot and dry.

"You need help, Maja," she insisted. "Come with me to my godfather,

---

*In Cuba, the maja is a nonpoisonous snake.

Mofá. Let him divine for you. Let him give you something to help you. You get sicker by the day."

Maja's wife was a believer in the orishas and the miracles their priests, the santeros, worked. Maja was a skeptic of the religion and all it entailed. He grumbled a bit, but he was so exhausted from his mysterious illness that he had not the strength to fight. With his wife he went to see the diviner.

Mofá divined: in Lucumí he prayed and questioned the orishas, casting the diloggún on the mat several times before speaking. "The orishas are not happy with you because you do not believe," he said, concerned. "Your illness, however, is not their doing. It simply is. But Obatalá stands up to save you. You need a rogación; this will cool your fever and restore your health."

"Obatalá wants me to make ebó? Who is this Obatalá? Show me! You cannot, for he is not real! I'm a sick man, and you want to cool my head with a rogación?" he breathed deeply calming himself. "Let my wife make ebó instead and cool her own head. I will seek out a doctor, and take medicine to rid myself of this illness."

Mofá sighed. "There is none more blind than he who refuses to see."

Maja's wife remained for a rogación. "It can't hurt," she told Mofá, and he shrugged his shoulders. Maja went home and called for the best physicians in Cuba to come to his bedside.

"This is most unusual," said one physician and the others agreed. That evening, they stayed with him; the fever grew. They administered medicines and remedies to bring it down, but it was to no avail. When his wife came home she was shocked. Her husband lay in bed, soaked in sweat, his fever so high he was delirious.

They worked all night to cool him and restore him.

Morning came and Maja's fever was lower but not broken; the physicians left, secure that he would recover. But as the day passed he became weaker. Soon his skin roughened and his extremities turned hard and blue. They were useless and Maja lay in bed, unable to rise. "Call the doctors," he cried to his wife. She ran from the house. He thought she was going to fetch a physician. The wife, however, went back to Mofá.

"He is dying," she cried to her godfather. "He is so weak that he cannot get out of bed."

Mofá divined again and worry twisted his face. "Your husband refused to make ebó," he told her, "and Obatalá is angry now. Your spouse sat here on the mat and made fun of him. He doubted his existence. A rogación will not help anymore. Obatalá says your husband must walk alone to a crossroads carrying a coconut and a white pigeon in each hand. Obatalá himself will come meet your husband, and Obatalá will restore him to health once he makes ebó."

She went home to tell him what Mofá said. When he heard her words, he roared. "Woman! I lay in bed unable to stand, and your witchdoctor wants me to walk? Is he crazy? Get me a doctor. And do it quickly before I die!"

There were tears in her eyes when she ran to fetch the doctors, and when they were on their way to her house she ran to get the items for ebó. "Perhaps if I go and explain to Obatalá my husband cannot walk," she reasoned, "he will have pity and save him."

At the crossroads she stood with one coconut and one white pigeon in each hand; she was there barely a minute when Obatalá himself rode by on his white horse. Before the orisha dismounted she was on the ground prostrating herself, her tears wetting the dust. Obatalá blessed her and hugged her.

"Father, my husband is dying. He cannot even walk. I came here with his ebó hoping that you would still save him." Her face was twisted with anguish when she pleaded, "Please save him."

Obatalá gave her a rogación and fed her orí in Maja's name. When he was done, he wrapped her head securely in white cloth, and told her, "Your husband has been sick too long, and he never made ebó for himself. His illness is too advanced. I might be an orisha, but I cannot break the natural laws Olódumare has set." She hung her head and began to cry again. "His arms and legs are dead; they died while you traveled here. I can't reverse that, but I can transform him into something new." He took her head in his hands gently, and tilted it so she looked him in the eyes. She felt such peace, and resigned herself to her husband's fate when Obatalá told her, "Your husband, Maja, will be known as the maja, and those who see him will scorn him as he has scorned me."

The woman thanked Obatalá, and ran home, her feet barely touching the earth. Her heart was in her chest when she burst through her own door, and she was gasping for breath when she went to her husband's bedside.

He was surrounded by several physicians, each with a look of horror on their faces.

For Maja's arms and legs died, and his body transformed. Maja was a snake, and frightening in his countenance. Thus was the snake known as the maja born on the island of Cuba.

Obatalá's Favorite Dove, or, How the Cat Lost His Dinner

From the Odu Okana Ogundá (1-3)

The color black will always fade and the color white will always stain.

Silently, the cat crouched low in the bush, watching the black pigeon as it hopped from branch to branch in a tree. His feline mouth watered, lips trembling slightly as his tail flicked quickly sideways. There was a slight rumble in his belly. "Sooner or later that bird will make a mistake, and when he does, he's mine," thought the cat.

Looking down from the tree, the black pigeon saw the tail end of a worm sticking out of the earth. He rustled his feathers excitedly, and dove down quickly. One swift tug of the worm and it was free, twisting and turning in his beak. One swift leap by the cat, and the pigeon was hanging loosely in his teeth, flapping his wings futilely.

The pigeon squealed in pain and fright, and the worm dropped, digging away into the earth. The cat mewed with satisfaction and hunger, and the black pigeon was free, flying to a distant house.

The cat growled angrily. "I'll get that black pigeon," he said, and he started to track the bird.

Obatalá was surprised when a black pigeon came hurtling through his window; so swiftly and quickly did it fly that it struck a wall, and bounced back onto the floor. "Poor bird!" Obatalá said, picking it up. "What a dirty bird!" he noticed, seeing the black mark it left on the wall, and the stain in his hands. Gently, Obatalá washed the black pigeon and was amazed when all the darkness washed away, leaving a white dove. The dark color was nothing more than dirt.

Groggily, the dove stirred in his hands. "Don't be afraid," soothed Obatalá. "You are safe."

Obatalá was an orisha, and as such, he understood the languages of all the animals. "The cat!" the bird screamed. "The cat is going to eat me."

"There is no cat here," insisted Obatalá.

He heard scratching at his front door. The bird flew to the top of the windowsill. "It's the cat, I know it," he whispered fearfully. "Please don't let him eat me."

Obatalá opened the door; and as the white dove feared, it was the cat, wanting to eat him.

"You have my dinner here, Obatalá," he accused.

"I have your dinner? I'm sorry, but I don't feed cats," said the orisha.

"I caught a pigeon in the woods, and it got away. I saw it fly into your window."

Obatalá took a deep, solemn breath; the cat watched his chest rise and fall. "I see," he said. "What color was your pigeon?"

"It was black. I want it now."

Obatalá smiled, "Dove, fly to me, please. It's okay. I won't let anyone hurt you."

The white dove flew down from its perch and landed on Obatalá's shoulder. "As you can see, cat, the only bird in this house is a white dove. It is my pet. Now if you'll excuse me, I have things to do, and I suggest you look elsewhere for your dinner."

In hunger, the cat left Obatalá's house, and the white dove lived his life safely.

The Birth of the Dead Sea
From the Odu Okana Odí (1-7)

The ocean feeds even the smallest pond
before water returns home again.

Yemayá Mayelewó lived alone in the ocean at the place where the seven great, watery tides met and mixed. Alone at the center of the sea, she contemplated herself each day. One day as she was lost in thought, it happened that Elegguá was swimming in the ocean, and he saw Yemayá lost in self-reverie. He decided to play a trick on her to see what she would do. Elegguá swam silently just beneath the water where Yemayá could not see him; he reached his hand above the surface and knocked her crown off her head. He sent it flying into the distance, toward land. Before Yemayá could spot him he dove deep into the ocean, deeper than even Yemayá herself could go. Immediately, Yemayá began to swim in circles, trying to find her crown; she looked up, and saw it spiraling off into the distance, as if launched by some great force. She knew not that it was Elegguá who had done this to her. It is for this reason that whenever Yemayá comes down, she dances in a circle; even now, when she comes down, she is looking for that lost crown.

She followed the crown's path; she swam as fast as she could, never taking her eyes off her lost treasure. Yemayá Mayelewó changed as she came closer to land; she turned into Yemayá Asesu, the orisha found behind the boulders near the shore. As she transformed, she lost sight of her crown but she knew it was somewhere on land. As she arose from the ocean, amphibious in form, she transformed again into Yemayá Ibú Ogúnté Ogúnasomí. This Yemayá walked the earth looking for her beloved crown. Soon, her seeking and searching took her miles and miles away from Nigeria; she was sad, for that crown was her most loved and coveted possession, and as depression overtook her she began to stab herself several times with her own knife. Her life's blood poured out of her, but Yemayá was an orisha, immortal, and could not die. Soon she gave up and headed back to the sea. But her blood remained covering the land, and that is how the Dead Sea was born.

How Osain Became an Herbalist
From the Odu Okana Ejila (1-12)

There are forests in heaven as there are
on earth, and both hold herbs for good
and evil.

Osain sat on the mat, watching intently as the diviner cast the òpèlè again and again. "Osain," Orúnmila said, "the forest holds danger for you. For the next seven days do not leave this house."

Osain smiled at Orúnmila, "I don't doubt your words, old friend, but I am the forest. I was born when the first blade of grass broke through the earth, and with each living tree that rose, I became stronger. What danger could the forest hold for me? I am its master."

"My words don't fall on the floor, Osain," Orúnmila warned. "Stay out of the forest. Better yet, just stay indoors."

He ended the divination session, kissing his òpèlè and tucking it safely in his pocket. Quickly, he gathered his things and was heading for Osain's door. Orúnmila's haste to leave was obvious to the orisha, and it bothered him. "Why are you in such a rush, Orúnmila," Osain asked. "Don't you like my company?" He smiled an annoyed smile.

Orúnmila needed to leave, but realized his quick exit might seem offensive to the orisha. He turned to face him. "I'm sorry, Osain. I didn't mean to be rude. Olófin called for me earlier today, and now I am off to heaven to divine for him."

"I have never been to heaven. Take me with you!"

Orúnmila looked at Osain, and his worry was obvious; it creased his brow and narrowed his eyes. "Did you not listen to a word I said to you? You are in danger, Osain. You have to stay home."

"You worry too much. What danger can there be in heaven? I will be with you and Olófin. How much safer could I be?"

Orúnmila was in a rush; he had no time to argue. "You are a creature of earth. The only way for you to travel with me to heaven is if I carry you, like I carry my bag."

"Not a problem for me," Osain said, jumping on Orúnmila's back. In moments, they were at Olófin's gates.

Orúnmila marked ebó for Olófin. "We need herbs to make omiero and a goat and a rooster for Eshu," Orúnmila told him. "That is the sacrifice you must make."

"It is wise to make ebó," agreed Olófin. "Please, find what you need, and I will reward you well for your work. Take Osain with you to help you."

So happy was Osain to be in heaven that he forgot about the warnings Orúnmila gave him, and Orúnmila was so focused on Olófin's ebó that he gave it not a thought. To save time the two orishas went out together to find the items needed for Olófin's ebó. Orúnmila went to the stables to find a goat, and Osain went to the forest to pick herbs. "Even in heaven," Osain said, "there are herbs and plants. This is just like the earth's forests."

Enchanted by the woods, Osain wasn't watching his step and he fell over a stray branch on the forest's floor; he fell, impaling his leg on another thick, sharp root that stuck up from the dirt. It tore his flesh, ripping a huge gash, and shattering the bone inside. Pain like hot fire shot up his leg and into his chest; he screamed, sending all the birds and small animals in the forest scrambling fearfully. Orúnmila heard his shriek and came running to his side.

When he got to Osain, he was lying in blood and gore.

"Help me," was all he said before fainting.

Days passed as Osain slept fitfully, trapped in the twilight just below consciousness. When he awoke, his leg was healing, but it was twisted and frozen in at an obscene angle. He couldn't bend it.

"What am I to do?" wailed Osain. Orúnmila looked at him pitifully. "How can I work and support myself if I can't walk like a normal man?"

Sadly, Orúnmila shook his head. "My friend," he said, sadly, "I told you my words don't fall on the floor. If you had listened, you would still have two good legs." A single tear slid down Osain's face while Orúnmila was lost in thought. "But in truth, I am just as responsible. After divining for you, I should have left you home. Wait: I will be right back."

Orúnmila left for some time, returning with a goatskin bag. Opening it, Osain saw it was filled with small packets of dried herbs, each labeled carefully. "These are all the medicinal herbs of the forest. There are twenty-one for every ailment humans suffer, and there are twenty-one for every sickness not yet born. Study these, Osain, for you can support yourself as an herbalist, healing the sick."

This is how Osain maimed his leg: This is how Osain became an herbalist. Everyone on earth sought the orisha for his cures.

2
PATAKÍS FROM THE COMPOSITES OF EJI OKO

The Story of Rain and Drought

From the Odu Ejioko Meji (2-2)

*When Drought is hungry, he is
not selective.*

Drought was an insatiable creature. He was born on a day when the earth was parched; it cracked as the sun rose in a cloudless sky. At first he was nothing more than a shimmer in the dry air or a puff of dust on the parched earth; but he was thirsty and nothing quenched that thirst. He sucked at the ponds and drank at the rivers drawing all the water he could find into himself. When everything was sucked dry, Drought lifted his arms to the sun; and gently he rose, spreading until he was huge, gaining strength from heat and covering the earth like a thick blanket. When sunset came on Drought's first day, the heat remained trapped and all living creatures suffered.

Drought was a vile creature; he knew that one day he would have the power to destroy the world. Had he a mouth with teeth, he would have smiled a wicked but toothy grin while trying to drink all the water on the earth.

So powerful was Drought that Rain himself was trapped in the invisible world as the earth suffered. Wasting no time, he went to see the diviner, Mofá. He was a wise man and if there was a way to replenish the earth and destroy the spirit known as Drought, he would find it.

"Mofá," he said to the diviner, "have you seen what this new creature, Drought, does on the earth? He's destroying it."

"Yes," said Mofá, "he has the waters of the world tied up and everything dries up."

"What can we do?"

"You can make ebó!"

"What ebó?"

Patiently, Mofá explained the ebó to his friend, Rain. "Bring me a goat," he said, "and bring me dozens of bolts of black cloth. I want razor-sharp knives and machetes, and all types of sharp things that you can find. Bring all this to me—for that is what the orisha Elegguá wants as ebó."

Rain scoured heaven looking for all those things. When he found everything he returned to the diviner. The world below looked parched and scorched. "How long can the world live like this?" Rain asked.

"Not long," he said. "Now go into the world. You are the rain, and only you have the ashé to overcome Drought."

Slowly, Elegguá feasted on the goat. He watched as Rain descended into the world; and he smiled as he became the rain. Light sprinkles and showers tickled the dirt and raised the dust. But Drought was too strong and the earth too dry; when the water hit land he sucked it up like it was never there, and the earth remained parched.

"I need help!" Rain screamed. His voice echoed through the cloudless skies. "Drought is too strong, and the world will die unless I defeat him!"

Elegguá finished his last bite of goat; and then he stood up and unrolled the black cloth across the sky. So dark was the cloth it blotted out the sun, and darkness spread. In the shadows Drought's heat subsided. Elegguá took a deep breath and blew across the earth; at first it was a gentle breeze and then a wild wind. The earth cooled. Rain spread himself through the sky with the black cloth and managed a few more drops of water, but his brother, Drought, was hiding in the earth and sucked those up.

"Take these," said Elegguá, handing the rain the bag filled with knives, machetes, and sharp objects. "Drought stands between you and the earth, and with these you can destroy him."

So Rain opened the bag and began throwing all manner of sharp things to the earth. In the air they transformed into great sheets of water that sliced through Drought, and they plunged deep into the earth. So great was the downpour that all living things took refuge in their homes. Even Drought hid, and the earth was replenished with the rain.

So it has been since that day: when Drought threatens to destroy the earth, Rain unfolds his black cloth across the sky and slices through until the earth is moist again.

The Birth of Rain
From the Odu Ejioko Owani (2-11)

The rain has no friends.

Her old body fought with the life inside her; it wanted to slide out, but so aged was she that her pelvis had not a clue how to relax and release. The midwife felt inside, two fingers sliding where five should have fit; she shook her head and coached the old woman, "Relax, and breathe."

"I feel like I'm dying and you want me to relax!" she screamed. Both hands were on her belly pushing; the sheets were soaked with sweat.

"You're not dying," crooned the midwife, trying to hide the worry in her voice. Her attempt was feeble at best. Her words caught in her throat and her voice rose an octave higher than it should. She focused on the old woman's pelvis. "Has she never had a child before?" she asked herself.

"But I am dying. A woman as old as I am should not have a child." She turned her head to the side, staring blankly at the walls. The pain subsided but the heaviness in her belly still pushed down on the unyielding pelvis. It ached. She wanted that ache to go away.

"Your body has been through this before. Just relax and let go." The midwife put a cloth to the old woman's forehead and wiped away the sweat that stung her eyes. Much longer and neither mother nor baby would live.

"I've never been through this before," she whispered, too weak for more than that. "This is my first child."

Those were the last words she spoke that night; words that left the midwife's mouth open the size of a deep yawn. "This is her first child? What is she? Almost fifty?" The old woman's eyes fluttered shut, and a sleep almost as deep as death came to her; mercifully, she felt no pain as her pelvis cracked and spread, freeing the child. The leathery skin between her legs ripped softly as the head pushed through, and then the shoulders; so in shock was the midwife that she barely caught the wet infant before the rest of its body slid from between the old woman's legs to the bed.

The boy born that night was a strange creature: it was feeble and frail like all newborns, its arms trembling with its first weak cries. He was born with skin darker than the blackest charcoal; and his eyes were pools of ink so thick there was no difference between his iris and pupils. Even the soles of his feet and hands were black, and the gentle folds of skin, which should have been lighter, matched the all-over darkness of his complexion. He had a thick head of curly hair coarser than a sheep's wool, more of it than a child three times his age. Only the whites of his eyes gave contrast to the dusky skin, and the whites were that of a snowcapped mountain, or a cumulous cloud hanging low against a clear blue sky. As his first cries twisted his face he seemed a caricature of a child, not real.

The midwife shuddered.

Relatives came later: aunts and uncles and brothers and sisters who lived in the surrounding villages. They were surprised when word was sent that she was having a child, her first child, and at her age. For even though she was the baby of her siblings, she was close to her half-century mark, way too old to be having children. The midwife was a wet nurse as well, thankfully, because the mother slept, weakened from giving birth. One by one her family passed the child among them, their eyes narrowing as they saw that the boy's skin was just too dark for a newborn. "Who is the father?" one of the male relatives asked.

The midwife shook her head as she took the boy from his arms. "I don't know. No one does except for her, and she's not talking."

They spoke of the child in whispers that night, laughing and taunting the old woman for giving birth at her age, and to a child so . . . dark. Unknown to them, she lay awake in the bed and smiled. From the next room she heard them; their words left her unfazed. He was her first son, her only son, and he was her pride and joy.

A mother's love is unconditional like that.

For years this old woman had been barren until she went to see the orisha priests and their diviners. With tears in her eyes but hope in her heart, she sat on the mat and listened patiently as the old men told her about her woe, and without her saying a word to them. They wrenched her heart for every word was true. When they explained her ebó it was not if she would make it, but when. It took some time but the old woman brought a black ram to be shared between Shangó and Yemayá and black male goat for Elegguá. She brought a bolt of black cloth and tubs of a black soap, and she carried a bag of machetes thrown over her shoulder. All this she brought; and after her ebó was complete she went home without tears but with faith.

Elegguá felt her sorrow more deeply than he should; both her empty heart and womb moved him that day. "She will bear a child," he promised her although he spoke not to her. "She will bear a child, and I will give him great ashé. Longing like hers to love another should not go unrewarded." Before she walked out of sight, Elegguá blessed her. Before long her womb was ripe with life.

And to her, the child born that night was miraculous.

She secluded him for years, and he was happy with his mother as his only friend. No one, not even her own family, got to see the child as he matured from an infant to a young boy; but children cannot be kept locked up out of sight forever, and the day came that he was expected to join other children for his lessons. She dressed him well in the finest of fabrics and sent him to his teachers. In school, he was taunted for the blackness of his skin.

Every day he came home from his lessons with tears; his clothing torn and his face twisted in a grimace of grief much too old for the face of a child to bear. It broke her heart, and it was not long before she believed that her ebó was a curse, not a blessing.

Elegguá saw all this. It angered him.

He came to the young boy; he found him sitting by the forest alone, tears streaking his face and making his skin both shiny and salty. When the child saw a man as black as he walking up to him he froze, and before the orisha could speak his little voice cracked as he asked, "You are as dark as me. Are you my father?"

Elegguá's heart broke. He had given the old woman a son, but he had forgotten to give him a father. He smiled and trembled just a bit as he said, "Yes. I am your father, in a way. Why do you cry?"

He clutched Elegguá's red and black robes, the tears flowing again, staining the cloth. "They say I'm too black. They say it's not natural. They hate me."

Elegguá knelt and held the young boy at arm's length by his shoulders; the child looked at the ground with shame, wiping tears from his eyes. "They're wrong," Elegguá said, shaking him gently so he would look up. "Do you hear me? They're wrong. Your blackness is a gift from Olódumare in heaven, and it is beautiful. It is also your power."

The child did not understand the concept of power; nor did he believe his blackness to be a gift. It was his curse, and he clutched the orisha Elegguá as he sat on the ground with him. All afternoon he cried and sobbed; and with each little wail, the sky rumbled. Clouds thickened, and gentle drops of water fell from them. The child did not notice them, so deep was his grief, but Elegguá did, and he thought, "Yes, your power will be great, indeed."

It was long after sunset before Elegguá brought the boy home. His mother was frantic with fear. "All the boys at his school are so mean to him," she thought in her panic. "Have they done something to him?" She was about to run out into the darkness screaming his name when he burst through the door, his little hand in Elegguá's. Together they marched in the house and sat on the floor, he in the orisha's lap.

She was about to scream with both fear and anger when Elegguá held up his hand to silence her. "Why?" he asked.

"Why what? Who are you? And where have you been, young man?" She pulled him away from the orisha who still sat on the floor grinning. She twisted him around and hugged him in her arms protectively. "Get out!" she told the orisha.

"You are angry with me?" Elegguá stood defiantly. "It is I who should be angry with you. This boy is tormented every day of his life. The boy for whom you prayed; the boy for whom you made ebó. Not once have you considered bringing him back to us . . . and making ebó for him. You really are quite a selfish woman."

"What?" her voice rose in pitch and cracked with that one word. Her son looked up at her curiously.

"What is power, Mama? He says I have it. And what is . . ." he formed his lips around the word carefully, "ebó?"

"How do you know these things?" She looked down at her son who was looking up at her. It was then she realized that his skin was as dark as the strange man's skin, the stranger who stood in front of her.

"Because I am Elegguá!" He held his arms out at his sides and bowed just a bit.

Her hands went to her mouth. Through her fingers she said, "Oh. My." Slowly, she tried to put her head to the floor, but before she could do more than bend at the waist Elegguá caught her.

"No need." He hugged her instead. When they stood at arm's length, she smiling at him, she said, "I need to thank you. He is my pride and joy. But the other children, even the other adults, are so mean to him. They say it is unnatural for a child to have skin and eyes and hair so black. But you . . ." her voice trailed off, ". . . but yours is just as black. How can this be?"

"That's not important," said Elegguá. "What is important is that we finish your ebó tonight. Years ago you began something very powerful, and now that power begins to manifest. After tonight, no one will ever taunt him again."

The young boy stared at Elegguá. Something primal stirred behind his eyes and his young mind knew the orisha's words were true. There was something powerful inside of him; it was growing as the adults spoke. He heard wind outside his home, and he knew, somehow, he made it blow. "Are you ready?" Elegguá asked.

The young boy shook his head. Thunder rumbled outside.

Throughout the night Elegguá put his ashé in the young boy. He ripped off his dirty clothes, cloth that was already ripped and torn by the beating his classmates had given him that day. Gently, he washed him with the black soap from head to toe, the dirty looking lather foaming and dripping over his thin, wiry body. Outside the winds continued to blow; they howled through the trees; and dirty clouds gathered in the night sky blocking out the moon and stars. Elegguá washed and lathered; washed and lathered; washed and lathered; and when the sun rose the next morning its light was muted by thick, black clouds that gathered and blocked out its light.

The world was afraid—something stronger than the sun was in the morning sky.

Elegguá rinsed the young boy's body with buckets of water; and gentle drops of rain fell from those clouds. The water crashed and slopped loudly in the metal washtub; and outside thunder rumbled through the sky.

People hid in fear from the strange noise.

While rain fell gently, and thunder rumbled hungrily, Elegguá dressed him in the black cloth. Outside the clouds grew even darker until the world was thrown into a twilight not unlike the moments before sunset. In spite of their fear, the villagers peered from their windows and wondered, "What evil is afoot?" Fathers hugged their wives; mothers hugged their children; and one by one families crept outdoors to have a better look at the strange things unfolding in their skies.

Finally, Elegguá gave the young boy two machetes. "You are ready to show the world who you are. Go out there and beat everything that stands in your way with these. No one will ever torment you again!"

With a smile on his face and lightness in his step, the boy, who was the Rain, did as he was told. He walked out the front door and started beating at the earth, the plants, and the trees that stood before him. Each strike brought lightning from the sky, fire that charred it but left him unharmed. The winds bore down from heaven pushing him each step of the way, and sheets of rain sliced through the sky, splashing and soaking the earth. Those who tormented him all his days, the boys and even their fathers, these he smacked with his machetes and watched them run in fear of the child who had fire in his eyes. And when he had shown everyone who ever tormented him his power, he lifted both arms to heaven and screamed—lightning, so bright it was blinding, flashed, and amid the wind and the rain and the thunder, he rose to heaven and took his place in the clouds.

His mother rejoiced that day, and for the first time the tears she cried over her son were not of sorrow, but happiness. For she had given birth to a powerful child, the Rain, and no one dared torment him again.

This is why we say that the rain has no true friends. For while he walked the earth as a mortal child, truly, he had no friends. And the water that falls from the skies, or the lightning that razes the earth, torments all equally and without discretion.

It made Elegguá very happy that day.

The Sickness of the Swamp
From the Odu Ejioko Owani (2-11)

*Without faith, not even the rain can
wash sickness away.*

The Mother of Rain sought out the diviners in heaven: not only did she want a child, but also she wanted a child of power; and not only did she want that child to be powerful, but also she wanted that child to have more power than anything on the earth. The diviners told her two things: make ebó and have faith. The Mother of Rain made ebó quickly, and she made it with faith in her heart; and she watched as her child's storm clouds unrolled over a clear, blue sky. She smiled as the clouds thickened and darkened the firmament. Her son had more power than the sun; he blocked out all of heaven and the earth sighed.

Rain came gently at first, and then he became a storm. Everything hid while sheets of water sliced the air. When the skies cleared and the sun bore down, it was humid and sticky. Creatures walked slowly on the earth's face, miserable in the clammy air. All the water that could ran to the river and the sea, but some was trapped in the moist earth where it became muddy and gooey; and as the water stood still, it stagnated. The swamp was born.

As those waters grew fetid, the swamp was sick. The Spirit of the Swamp went to the diviners to make ebó.

"If you want your health back," the diviners told him, "you must make ebó. More importantly you must have faith. For ebó without faith is as futile as not making ebó at all."

In spite of the decay and decomposition developing in his own body, the swamp found the strength to make ebó; but he did it with hopelessness in his heart and not faith. To the orishas he gave roosters and hens and all types of four-legged animals, and he served his own head with the same. When he was done he sank back into his fetid waters and waited for death to come.

Instead of death the rain came again; and when the sky cleared, his swamp was more putrid than before.

He sighed a deep sigh as he resigned himself to a life of suffrage: because he made ebó, he was immortal on the earth, but because he had no faith his sickness remained. And this is why even today the swamps are filled with disease and decay while the waters of the world remain fresh; and over all these the Rain has power because his Mother in heaven made ebó for him.

3
PATAKÍS FROM THE COMPOSITES OF OGUNDÁ

Why the Cat Is Chased But Not Caught
From the Odu Ogundá Meji (3-3)

Treason comes from those who profess most loudly that they are friends.

"Teach me to climb trees," the cat heard someone say as she lay on a tree branch high above the forest.

She dug her claws in the green wood to keep her balance, leaning her head over to see who spoke. It was a dog; he looked up at her panting silently, his tail wagging rapidly back and forth. "You're a dog," said the cat. "Dogs don't climb trees."

"Oh but we could," said the dog. "And we'd be good at it if we had someone like you to teach us."

The cat sighed and closed her eyes. Dogs and cats were not

friends. More than once she herself had fled from them, finding safety only when she scaled the trunk of a tree, hiding high in its branches. If a dog knew how to climb a tree there would be no place safe for any cat to hide. "Still," she thought, "this dog might prove useful."

"And what will you give me in return for my knowledge?" asked the cat. "For surely, climbing trees is a skill that would come in handy for anyone. It is valuable knowledge. What would you give me in return?"

The dog frowned. "What do you want?"

The cat was silent while she thought long and hard. "I want to hunt." She saw the puzzled look on the dog's face. "Oh, sure, I can hunt. Any animal in the forest can. But I live off rats and mice, and sometimes birds. I want to know how to track and kill larger prey. I might never be able to take down a deer or even a fox, but there are larger animals that I could eat: some my size or larger. Teach me how to track and kill those, and I will teach you how to climb trees."

"Agreed," said the dog. He began teaching the cat that afternoon.

Days passed; the cat watched the dog hunt—she watched his every move. He taught her how to sniff at the earth. "Each animal has its own scent, and if you are observant, you can tell the difference between them." He taught her how to identify animals from their footprints in the soft earth. "Each animal has its own unique print," he said, "and if you put your paw in a track and it is more than twice the size of your own, the animal is too big for you to kill." He showed her how to hide in the bushes, how to move silently and in shadows, and how to pounce so she landed on her prey's back. "If you bear down on their back and hold tight, they cannot shake you off," he said. He taught her the softest parts of each animal's body, places where a well-placed claw would mortally wound or even kill her prey.

When he taught her all he knew, he asked the cat, "Now will you teach me to climb trees?"

"Not just yet," said the cat. She knew how to hunt, but she had yet to practice her skills; and she was no fool. The cat knew that if the dog could climb trees, none of her kind would ever be safe. "You've taught me much but I've practiced little. You must give me time to assimilate all the new skills you've taught me."

The dog growled and crouched; he was an impatient creature. As the cat's fur rose and she backed away he recomposed himself quickly. The cat froze where she stood, ready to flee. "Very well, my friend," he said. "We will hunt together."

The cat relaxed and went off with the dog, but now, she no longer trusted him.

They spent days hunting in the forest, the dog taking down large animals while the cat mastered killing things twice her size. Together they sat down each evening to eat their kill—the dog ripping into his while the cat nibbled hers delicately. As predators they roamed the forest, and as predators they bonded. Some days the cat was able to forget that the dog tormented her kind; and the dog forgot that his kind chased and killed cats. But the day came that the hunting went poorly and the cat was the only one to kill prey. Hunger overwhelmed the dog, and in a moment of anger he pounced on the cat. She dropped her meal and slashed the dog with her claws before scrambling up a tree.

With her gone, the hungry dog ate her meal. When his hunger was sated he realized the cat was gone.

He sniffed the earth until he found the tree in which she hid. "My friend," he called out to the cat as she clung to the branches high above his head, "I am sorry. I was overwhelmed with hunger. Please come back down; I won't hurt you. And you still have to teach me how to climb trees!"

"You're crazy!" howled the cat. "And I'm so glad that I never taught you how to climb trees. For if I had, I would be dead right now, as is the game I caught. I knew you were not to be trusted. And now I know all you know about hunting; and you know absolutely nothing about climbing a tree. You're a fool, dog."

Since the day that the cat and the dog betrayed each other they have remained enemies; yet the cat, because she was the smarter of the two, is always chased but never caught.

How the Cat and the Ferret Became Enemies
From the Odu Ogundá Irosun (3-4)

The trap will be paid for by blood.

It was midnight and the moon's pale crescent barely lit the darkness. Still, it was enough light for the ferrets' keen eyes as they crept from the forest to the farm. Across the well-trimmed grass they scurried toward the henhouse, quietly so the rooster would not hear them and sound an alarm. There were dozens of them, their dark bodies moving in waves that seemed to make the dark earth ripple and boil with shadows. An occasional ferret would break the march, standing on his hind legs to better sniff at the night air—the scents and smells coming downwind from the coop were almost hypnotic to their keen noses—but another ferret would quickly overrun him, forcing him back on all fours to keep up the silent march. In just minutes they formed a circle around the henhouse; it was a sea of ferrets, predators with one thing on their minds—food.

In mass they swarmed the front door. Before the rooster woke up to see what was happening, dozens of his hens were already dead, their necks sliced by the ferrets' sharp teeth and claws. Some they strangled by wrapping their long bodies around their heads and necks. They grabbed them with their teeth and dragged their lifeless bodies through the night, back to the forest.

In panic the rooster crowed. It was loud and shrill. He sounded several warnings, flapping and pecking at the ferrets that remained behind before they were able to slice his own neck. They left the rooster sitting there, gurgling and writhing in his own blood. Rooster meat was tough; none of the ferrets wanted to eat him.

By the time the farmer grabbed his machete and his lantern, they were gone and with them the bodies of his hens. He tapped the rooster with the toe of his shoe. When it lay still he knew it was dead.

The farmer was beyond angry.

The ferrets knew they would be blamed for the attack but they had a plan. Back at their den they ripped the feathers from the hens' carcasses, packing all these into a bag. Just before sunrise they were outside the cat's house. They dumped the feathers at her front door, and they watched as the gentle night breezes lifted and scattered them through her yard. Satisfied that this was proof enough that the cat had done the deed and not them, the ferrets ran home. Later today they would feast, gorging themselves on chicken.

Of all the animals that lived near town, the farmer knew the ferret was the one most likely to raid his henhouse. That morning he gathered all his neighbors; they were farmers themselves, and with machetes drawn they went to the ferrets' den. As they approached they saw a single ferret keeping watch; all the others were inside preparing their meal. The angry farmer was at the lead; his face twisted with rage. The ferret showed no fear.

"Where are my chickens?" It was an accusation, and his voice was loud. It cracked with anger.

"What chickens?" asked the ferret. He showed no emotion.

"My chickens!" The farmer trembled where he stood, his knuckles growing white as he gripped the machete's blade. "Last night some of your kind came around my henhouse and killed all my hens. You stole them. I want them back, dead as they might be."

The ferret raised himself up on his hind legs to look more imposing. "If we have your chickens, sir, then why aren't there any feathers?" The farmer's posse looked around. There were no feathers in sight. "We're not the neatest creatures, as you know. When we eat, we make a mess. If we had your chickens here surely you would see feathers."

"Who would see what feathers?" asked another ferret as he came outside, shutting the door behind him quickly. The farmer tried to see past the door, but it was too dark inside, and the ferret was too fast closing the door. "What feathers are we talking about?"

"The feathers of my chickens!" The ferret noted that the farmer's eyes were red as if he had not slept all night. "Your kind stole my chickens last night."

"I take offense at that," said the second ferret. "There are no chickens here. There aren't even any chicken feathers here. Why don't you go see the cat? As you know . . . cats love chicken."

"We should go," said one of the other men, putting a hand firmly on the farmer's arm. "We should go see the cat. The ferret is right. If they had stolen all your chickens last night there would be feathers. Lots of them. There are none here."

The farmer glared one last time as he backed away; and the group left their den to go see the cat. When they were gone another ferret peered out the front door. "They're gone? Good. Dinner is served!" The three ferrets scurried back inside the house.

The farmer cried when he saw the cat's yard littered in feathers. And when he saw the cat playing among them, his anger returned. He lifted his machete above his head and screamed but the others held him back. "Wait," said one of the men. "This is too obvious. It doesn't seem right."

The cat froze when he heard the farmer scream, and when she saw the machete high above his head, she cowered. One of the men walked up to her. "Don't be afraid, not unless you're the one who stole the farmer's hens."

"What?" cried the cat. "I haven't stolen anything."

"But your yard is littered in feathers," said the farmer. "Last night all my hens were stolen and their feathers are here. And you are playing in them."

The cat sat back on her haunches, whipping her tail at a feather that flew too close to her face. "I woke up this morning to find my yard covered in feathers. I've been playing in them all day. But there are no chickens here. Feel free to look inside my house if you don't believe me, farmer."

He and his men did just that—they walked through the cat's house. Inside were neither feathers nor meat. They came back out. "Then how do you explain all these feathers, cat?"

"I don't know. Certainly if all your chickens are gone you don't think I did it. I'm but a single cat. Your hens numbered in the dozens. Nor do I care who did it, as arrogant as you are. You have some nerve to come at me, an innocent cat, with a raised machete! But if your chickens were stolen last night, they're probably being eaten today. Find the bones and then you will have your thief."

"Those tricky, tricky ferrets," said the farmer, the anger rising in him again. "They kept sliding in and out of their front door never letting us see what was inside. And they sent us here, to the cat. They are the thieves!"

"The ferrets?" asked the cat. "But the ferrets and I are friends. Why would they steal your hens and bring their feathers here?"

"Obviously they're not your friends, cat. If you'd like to go with us you may. If they have the chickens, I'm sure you'll have a few questions for them as well."

"Indeed I will," said the cat as she followed the farmers back to the ferrets' den.

Back at the ferrets' den no one kept watch at the front door. Silently the farmer and the cat crept close; they stood outside the door listening. They heard laughter, and the sounds of dozens of ferrets enjoying an afternoon meal. "They are feasting on something," said the cat.

"Probably my hens," growled the farmer.

From inside the door they heard a ferret say, "I need some fresh air.

Don't eat all the chickens while I'm gone!" The cat and the farmer stood on either side of the door, and when it opened, the farmer grabbed the ferret by the scruff of its neck.

"Go inside and see if they have my hens!" he ordered while the ferret struggled to get free.

Before the cat could rush inside there was a great scream and dozens of ferrets came rushing out the door. Even though the ferrets swarmed the front door, the cat could see over them; there were the hens—roasted and baked—their carcasses strewn about the inside of the den. "Your hens!" she cried. "They have your hens!"

The farmer wrung the neck of the ferret he held; it went limp and lifeless. The cat managed to slash a few with her claws. "How dare you all set me up!" she screamed as she mortally wounded a few. The other farmers slashed with their machetes, but most of the ferrets ran off into the forest, too afraid to look back.

When all the ferrets were gone the farmer sat with his back against the den; the cat curled next to him, and the other men gathered around them sorrowfully. "I am sorry I blamed you, cat."

"Apology accepted. But you know that the ferrets will be back when you've replenished your coop. None of your hens will be safe."

"How would you like a job?" the farmer asked the cat.

It was that day that the cat went off to live in the farmer's barn; she kept watch at night for the ferrets, who were now her enemies, and the farmer pampered her well. She never wanted for a place to sleep or food to eat. And the ferrets, who were now known to be thieves, were forced to live in the forests and deserts all their lives. Instead of stable homes, they were forced to wander like gypsies from place to place.

But this is what happens when one steals what is not his, and this is what happens when one tries to set another up to take the blame for his own crimes.

Where the Goat Was First Sacrificed
From the Odu Ogundá Unle (3-8)

*Ogundá (Ogún) binds the blessed head
and puts Unle (Obatalá) in place.*

It was almost midnight and the full moon cast a silvery light on the gates of Ido. The town slept. It was not the peaceful slumber of innocents, but an exhausted sleep brought on by greed and excess. Olófin stood just outside those gates peering in, shaking his head woefully. Ido was beautiful once, a clean, prosperous city filled with joyous laughter. Now it was dirty, a dry shell of what it once was, its beauty shed like an old snakeskin and its laughter replaced by sorrow. The youth had risen up and driven the elders out of town; they pillaged and plundered the wealth accumulated by years of labor; and now they squandered it on immoral pleasures.

From the path leading to the city came a faint light; Olófin turned and watched as it came closer. In its warm glow he saw the white robes and wrinkled, wizened face. It was Obatalá; slowly he walked toward Olófin. In one hand he held a lantern and with the other he gave Olófin a light hug.

"It is good to see you, Obatalá," he said, returning the embrace carefully to avoid the hot lantern that floated between them.

"And it is good to see you, Olófin." Concern deepened his wrinkles. "Why are we here outside the gates of Ido?"

"I wanted you to see what it has become."

"What it has become? It is a great city! What more could it achieve?"

"Just look, Obatalá, and see for yourself." Olófin's voice trailed off into the chilled night air. Obatalá tilted his head, puzzled.

Olófin stepped to the side as Obatalá lifted his lantern to the side and above his shoulders; his ancient eyes narrowed as he looked past the gates. With the full moon's soft phosphorescence he was able to see the city in a silvery relief; it seemed to shimmer under its glow. But while the light was beautiful, what it illuminated was not. He saw the littered streets, unkempt, and the houses and storefronts with broken doors. A gentle wind wafted through the night lifting the scent of decay; Obatalá's nostrils widened and then snapped shut. "What happened here?" He turned to Olófin, bringing his lantern down so quickly that it almost slapped him in the face. "Ido . . . what happened to it?"

A deep sigh, and with it Olófin's chest lifted and lowered slowly. "What always happens, Obatalá? A group of hardworking humans settle a town. They marry; they have families, and they work hard to be prosperous. And then their children decide 'we know better than they do,' and they try to improve on what their elders set down." He paused, peering back through the gates. "Only this time it was worse. There was a revolt, a terrible uprising by the town's youth, and they drove all the elders away. You are looking at a town of children run by its youth."

"A town cannot be governed by its children, not without their elders to advise them. They will destroy themselves."

"They already have," said Olófin. "Ido is all but in ruins."

"They need their elders back," said Obatalá. "They need their wisdom, their life experience. We must quell the uprising first and install a temporary ruler. I will go out into the world and find the elders who fled. I will lead them back. And once we enter the town again as a group, I will make ebó so that this never happens again."

Olófin smiled. Obatalá was such a forgiving orisha that it melted his heart. He had been ready to smite the town, reduce it and everyone inside its gates to cinder and ash. He had only called Obatalá here to witness the town's evil before he wiped it clean. Yet Obatalá's words moved him; they stirred his heart and quenched his desire to destroy. Perhaps if he told him the full story—that those who ruled now wiped out those who ruled before, that they murdered them in cold blood and in their sleep—perhaps he would not be so quick to forgive. Or perhaps it would kill him. Or maybe he would forgive all the same.

Olófin decided to keep the full story to himself; already Obatalá was overwhelmed with grief. It was too much for the old man to handle. "Your forgiveness is deep and unconditional, Obatalá. I would be lying if I did not tell you I was going to destroy this city this very night. I only wanted you here to see what state it was in before I rose up and brought it down."

"Father, no!" The old man fell to the earth and put his head to Olófin's feet; the lantern, dropped, lost its light. "They are young. They are reckless, yes, but they deserve a chance. Let me find the elders and bring them back. Let me make ebó. Humans are, basically, good creatures."

Olófin bent down and touched Obatalá's shoulders lightly; he lifted him and the two embraced. There without the lantern's light, among the darkness and the shadows and pale moonlight, they embraced, and tears fell freely from their eyes. "You are too forgiving, Obatalá. I will give you one chance to make this right."

Obatalá shook his head gingerly; he gathered up the hem of his robes and walked off into the darkness. His sadness darkened the road he traveled. Olófin stood still at the town's gates. When Obatalá was out of sight, he called to the warriors Elegguá and Ogún. Together the two orishas had been waiting in the forest. "You know what to do?" he asked them.

"Yes, Olófin, we know," said Elegguá.

"No one is to get in, Elegguá," ordered Olófin.

"No, father, no one will get past me."

"And if anyone escapes this night with his life, let him leave. Let him leave in fear to tell the world of how Ogún destroyed them all for their evil ways! There must be people left alive to tell the story of Ido so humans are loath to repeat its history. But if any tries to come back?"

"If any dare come back," said Elegguá, "it's off with his head!"

"No one comes back," repeated Olófin. "No one except Obatalá, and whatever elders he might find in the world who will want to come back." He turned to Ogún; already the warrior was clutching his machetes in both hands so tightly that the muscles in his arms bulged and twitched.

"It begins. It begins now!" ordered Olófin, and Ogún growled like a hungry beast. With glazed eyes he marched through the darkened town, Olófin at his heels. By sunrise the leaders of the revolt were dead, murdered in their sleep, their blood shed like a great sin offering to Olódumare in heaven above. Their harlots, their whores—these, too, lay dead in their embrace. The older among them who worked as soldiers in their army fled, some finding death on the edge of a machete before they could make it to the streets while others were able to flee past the gates, Elegguá laughing gaily as he watched them run in fear. When the sun was strong in the morning sky, children lined the streets wiping the sleep from their eyes. They cried when they saw Ogún's dreadful form clutching bloodied machetes; but Olófin directed Ogún back to the gates and waited while their cries subsided.

"You're safe now," Olófin said, shaking his heads at their dirty, unfed bodies. One by one he took care of them, the oldest of the children helping with the youngest. When the sun set on that first day, there was some semblance of order back in the town. When the children were tucked into a bed in a makeshift camp, Olófin sighed. "It is a town of children," he thought. "They need their elders to raise them." He left the oldest in charge and went to find Elegguá and Ogún at the town's gates.

There at the gates Olófin found Elegguá and Ogún standing guard. Ogún was calm now, the blood lust that fueled his divinely murderous rage quelled to a mild heat, and Elegguá stood with him, calming him, whispering words in his ear that seemed to unglaze his eyes bit by bit. When Elegguá heard Olófin's approach, he put a gentle hand on Ogún's back and turned to face the ancient one.

"How is he?" Olófin asked. His eyes were teary. Ogún was a frightful creature when divine vengeance filled his heart; and when his hands were stained with blood, he was impossible to calm. Like a forest fire he had to burn himself out before the anger was gone, and even then, hot embers burned, embers that could spark another rage at any moment. Olófin hated using Ogún's ashé for divine bloodshed, but in times like these there was no other way to right a wrong and restore balance in the world. It was part of Ogún's nature, and part of the reason Olódumare created him. He noted the sheen of sweat on his hard body, the rapid rising and falling of his chest, and the bloodstained hands.

The stains were fresh. Elegguá saw Olófin staring at them. "He would be calm by now had not several of the youth tried to come back. As you instructed, we chopped off their heads as they entered the town." Elegguá pointed behind a bush and Olófin saw the heads stacked neatly like blocks, and then he saw the bodies lying just outside the gates. "We left their bodies where they fell," said Elegguá.

"How long has it been?" he asked.

Elegguá thought for a moment. "The sun was still high in the sky when they tried to overcome us. They all came together, one large band of humans. They saw only two of us compared to a dozen of them. They thought they could take us."

"Foolish," said Olófin, and then, "I'm exhausted. I've directed Ogún all night, and I've cared for children all day." As the night deepened and the stars winked overhead, Elegguá and Olófin stood watching Ogún. The night calmed him; and anger slipped off his shoulders like a scarf blown away in the wind. He relaxed, sat down, and fell over in a deep sleep. "Watch him, Elegguá. I don't think anyone else is foolish enough to come back. Hopefully they've scattered throughout the world to tell their tales of woe. I doubt the massacres of Ido will happen again, at least not for a while. I'm going to bed myself."

"Wait." Elegguá reached out for Olófin's shoulder before he could walk away. "What if others do try to come back? What do you want us to do?"

"Cut off their heads, of course. Let no one back in."

"But what if innocents come through?"

"No one innocent travels in darkness, Elegguá. In the morning

I want you to go out into the world and let everyone know that the gates to Ido are sealed. Anyone who comes this way will find death as a punishment from me. Ogún will stand guard at the gates and decapitate those who try to come. And I will watch over the children until Obatalá returns with the elders. If they choose to come back."

Olófin walked back to the camp where the children were sleeping. Eleggúa's heart was sorrowful as he watched him slip into shadows. He sat beside Ogún and watched the gates.

No one tried to return.

While Olófin was directing Ogún's army to kill Ido's revolutionaries, Obatalá was walking into the world, looking for the banished elders of Ido. When the sun rose the next day, while Olófin tended the village's children, Obatalá was gathering the elders together, telling them what he found in the once great city and begging them to return to their children.

"How can we return, Obatalá?" the eldest of the men asked him. "These children murdered our king and our queen in their sleep; and they murdered the royal children as well. Everyone in the palace found death while they slept: death at the end of a machete or even a knife. Those youth in power now are cunning, and they are evil. They will destroy us if we return."

"We were lucky to escape with our own lives!" said the eldest woman. "While we fled the town arrows flew. Some of us were struck in the back, and we lived," she said pointing to her own back. Beside her shoulder blade was a wide, thick bloodstain. "Others of us fell down dead while we ran. These new leaders are not children. They are monsters."

Obatalá's heart froze in his chest. He heard the fear in their voices; he saw the fear in their eyes. Olófin had spared him the whole story. "But you still have children there," said Obatalá. "You have grandchildren there. They need their elders."

"Can you restore law and order?" asked another man. "Can you assure us that we will return to Ido and be safe?"

"I can," said Obatalá. "We will return as a group. Olófin is there; Olófin is restoring order as we speak. And once we are back in Ido I will make ebó so that this never happens again."

The eldest man spoke again. "Gather the things for your ebó, Obatalá. If you can do these things, we will return with you. We believe in you. We will walk with you to Ido and take back what belongs to us."

Obatalá smiled and he spent the rest of the day gathering what he needed for ebó. When finally he fell into a deep slumber, there was, again, a semblance of joy in his heart.

Joy did not last long.

The next morning everyone in the village awoke to a strange little man dressed in red and black; he was wiry and spry, running through the town like a demented child. As he ran recklessly he yelled, "Death to all who enter Ido! Death to all who enter Ido!"

Obatalá was the first to recognize him. "Eshu!" he called out. "Why do you say that?"

Eshu ran to Obatalá and threw himself at his feet briefly, waiting for him to touch his shoulders and bless him. Obatalá did; Eshu jumped up as if he had springs on his feet. "Because Olófin says that all who enter Ido will find death. They will lose their heads." With those words he ran through the town announcing, "Death to all who enter Ido!" It was almost a chant, and his words died in the distance as Eshu ran out of that town and into the next.

"You see?" said the eldest of the elders. "We cannot go with you. The town is locked down and anyone who goes there finds death."

"Call for us once you are there," said the eldest woman. "If you go to Ido and make ebó, and if you can restore order, call for us. But we have suffered enough. We will not go back unless it is safe."

The crowd of elders agreed with the eldest; Obatalá felt the fear in their hearts. It was real and it was deep. Sadly he shook his head in agreement. "I will go alone. I will make ebó. And when it is safe, I will send for you all."

That morning Obatalá gathered his things and started the day's journey back to the gates of Ido. He had not walked far before the weight of the ebó he carried tired him, and he sat down to rest.

As he rested, he spied a goat lulling in the bush; mindlessly, it grazed on the wild grasses. For quite some time Obatalá watched the goat, and when the animal finally raised his head and spied the old man, he smiled. "Obatalá!" he said, lowering his head to the ground in subservience, "it is a pleasure to see you here."

Gently the orisha tapped him on his shoulders and bid him to rise. The goat saw the huge load sitting at the orisha's feet. He frowned. "Why do you carry such a heavy load, Father?" he asked. "Is that why you sit here tired and resting?"

Obatalá nodded his head. "The burden I carry is huge, goat. Olófin entrusted me with making ebó on behalf of Ido. It is a town besieged by evil. After I make ebó, the evil will be quelled, and all the elders can return to their children."

The goat knew little about ebó, but he loved Obatalá dearly, as did most creatures on the earth. His kindness and gentle nature were well known. "Father, let me carry your burden for you. I am young and I am strong. You can tie it to my back, and you, as well, can ride. I will carry you to the town of Ido."

He was happy to let the animal help. Carefully Obatalá tied his huge load to the goat's back, and then he mounted as well. Together they traveled the road to Ido.

While Eshu ran through the world warning everyone about the town of Ido, Elegguá was sitting by the city's gates keeping watch, and Ogún slept fitfully, his hands still brandishing the machetes. When Obatalá and the goat rose in the distance like two faint dots, Elegguá saw them; but because Obatalá's clothes were soiled from his journey, and because he sat on the back of a goat with huge saddlebags, Elegguá did not recognize him as an orisha.

Elegguá shook Ogún. "Wake up, Ogún. There is someone coming to the gates of Ido now." The orishas hid on either side of the gates,

Elegguá holding a basket to catch the head while Ogún stood brandishing his machete high above his head. They waited silently; and it was
the goat's head that crossed the gate first.

With one powerful swoop, Ogún brought the machete down; the
goat's head, severed from its body, fell in the basket Elegguá held; and
slowly, its body collapsed under Obatalá's legs. Obatalá planted his feet
firm on the earth as the goat fell lifeless beneath him, and he watched,
with horror as first Ogún and then Elegguá drank the blood that
sprayed from the neck like a fountain. When they were done Elegguá
lifted the basket with the head and presented to Obatalá, and Obatalá,
still in shock, stood there holding it.

Olófin came to the gate that morning after the goat was killed; he
saw Ogún and Elegguá prostrated on the earth before Obatalá, and
he saw Obatalá holding the basket with the head. He smiled. "So be
it," he said, "that Obatalá himself will be the head of this town, and
all who come will pay him homage." Gently he took the basket from
the old man's hands and embraced him. "And while the world is still
a world, the goat, for disobeying my orders, will be sacrificed for all
those who savor his meat."

The white goat became the favored sacrifice of Obatalá that day; and
when war arises in any land, it is the sacrifice of that between he, Ogún,
and Elegguá that wins the war. One by one, all the elders of Ido returned
to care for its youth; they taught them the ways of the world and how to
be prosperous. And Obatalá remained as its spiritual head, the advisor
to all the kings and queens who ruled the town with wisdom.

4

PATAKÍS FROM
THE COMPOSITES
OF IROSUN

The Sun, the Moon, the Fire, and the Water

From the Odu Irosun Meji (4-4)

If the diloggún is not consulted,
one does not know his destiny;
and even if one knows

his destiny, without ebó it is
nothing.

The moon set and the sun had yet to rise. Campfires died until there were only embers; soon even those were gone, and there had been no rain in days. In that thick twilight before morning, darkness swathed the earth like rich, black velvet, and in its midst stood four umbrous figures. They were the spirits enlivening the sun, the moon, the fire, and the water. While standing on earth as shadows, the elements they ruled slept; and there they formed a motionless circle. Their only light was that of a thousand pale stars, useless but still comforting as they hung in the sky.

Everything was quiet; the only sounds were their breaths, deep and hollow. The silence was strained—for days the four spirits argued about who was the greatest and who had the most ashé. Their arguments proved futile, and one by one they went to see the diviners in heaven. Now, they waited on earth.

After a time, a gentle luminescence rose between them; at first it was a subtle glow, almost imperceptible, but it grew and chased the shadows away. Something took shape inside that light, and the four figures stood in the presence of an old man, Olófin. One by one they bowed, putting their heads to the ground while waiting for him to bless and lift them. Stiffly he moved: lovingly he embraced each.

The old man smiled at each of them. With a voice too youthful for his aged form he said, "It is time to settle your arguments. Have you made your ebós?"

"I have!" The first spirit who spoke was the sun, and the other three forms fidgeted nervously. "I made my ebó—I was first, and I know I will be the most powerful! It is my destiny to light the day-time sky, to bring light and warmth and joy to the world Olódumare created."

Of course it was a lie. While in heaven the sun had gone to the diviners before he came to earth, and the old men in heaven told him that his power would be great. "You are the ball of light in the sky, the one who destroys the darkness and warms the world. It is your destiny to be powerful. Still, to ensure your place and power in nature you must make ebó. You must sacrifice to Elegguá."

All the sun heard was, "It is your destiny to be powerful."

"If that is my destiny," he reasoned, "then there is no need to make ebó!"

Olófin smiled, but weakly. He knew it was a lie. The sun had not made ebó, but he said nothing. "And the rest of you? Have you all made ebó?"

"I made my ebó," said the spirit who was the moon. "And there is more to power than raw strength, Sun. Mine is the light that shines in darkness; I am she who inspires poets to write and lovers to love. I bring magic, mystery, and romance into the world. Therein lies true power."

It was a lie—the moon had not made ebó. As had the sun, she went to see the diviners and they told her, "Your power is great. You inspire poets and lovers and dreamers. To lock in your good fortune and your ashé, you must make ebó to Elegguá." The moon heard only this, "Your power is great," and she paid no mind to the ebó she needed to offer Elegguá.

Olófin smiled again, weakly. The moon's dishonesty concerned him but he said nothing. "And you? Have you made ebó?" He looked at the spirit who was the fire.

He puffed his chest up proudly, beating it with his fist when he said, "I have made my ebó, Olófin. Of all gathered here, it is I who am the most powerful. I will become the fire in the storm, the lightning that flashes from sky to earth. I will become the fire that warms men on cold, moonlit nights, and I will be the fire that cooks their food during the day when the sun shines. And I will be the fire that consumes and destroys when the hearts of men become cold and angry. That is true power."

Of course the fire lied as well. In heaven the diviners told him to feed Elegguá a goat, three roosters, and a guinea hen; but that seemed like too much trouble to the fire. Instead he offered Elegguá a single rooster before leaving heaven. He was in a rush; he had no time to make ebó. Fire was rash like that, always moving and never thinking.

Once again Olófin smiled, but in the pale light the shadows deepened it into a frown. A partial ebó was as good as no ebó, and sometimes, for teasing the orisha Elegguá, it was even more dangerous. "And what about you?" He turned to the creature that was the water. "Have you made your ebó?"

Shyly, looking at her feet, she said, "Yes, Father. I have made ebó.

Eleggúa asked for a bolt of dark cloth and a bag of sharp things—knives and machetes. He asked for a goat and a rooster and a guinea hen. I have given him all for which he asked."

Olófin smiled; it was deep and radiant. "As you have made ebó, so will you be blessed." As quickly as he came, Olófin's light winked out; and the darkness was instant. It seemed their eyes snapped shut, and ghostly lights danced in their vision before the night swallowed them up.

The spirits who were the sun, the moon, and the fire fidgeted nervously while the water felt her way through the night. She remembered her own time on the mat with the diviners. Their words to her were simple, "Of all the elements, you are the one most stable and the one most delicate. Your power will be simple—to refresh the world." She thought to herself, "My power is to be simple when I am surrounded by so much greatness." It was disheartening; but still, she made ebó. Now that she knew the diviners promised the sun, the moon, and the fire great power, she chose to leave and not watch as they received their ashé. And she would receive her own ashé alone, far away from them all, if at all.

When water was gone into the shadows, the sun turned to the fire. "She left. The water left. She is too weak to stand with us; she fears our power. Did you really make ebó?"

"Of course I did." His voice wavered. "Did you?"

"Didn't all of us?" asked the moon. Her voice was soft and unsure.

"When do we settle this?" asked the sun. He was impatient.

"Now!" said Eleggúa. The orisha stood hidden in shadows; no one knew he was there listening the entire time. Darkness melted like thin sheets of ice as the moon gave off a pale, silvery light; slowly she rose until she was floating high above the earth.

"She did make ebó," said the sun.

"Didn't you?" asked the fire.

The earth was covered with a light luminescence. The water, who had walked some distance away, looked up at the sky and sighed. "Her ebó must have been great. She is beautiful." She kept walking, her footsteps easier in the silver light.

A thin sheen of sweat rose on the sun's brow as he felt heat rising in his belly; he held out his arms—they were glowing. Warmth and light grew until he was lighter than the air; slowly, he lifted off the ground until he floated in the crack between the earth and sky. Bit by bit he slid up the eastern horizon; the sunrise that morning was brilliant, so brilliant that he paled the moon's soft glow. He stood in the east as she sank in the west and he yelled to her, "My power is great! I shine brighter than you, moon!"

The water stopped again and watched the sunrise; she watched until the sun's light hurt her eyes. "His ebó must have been greater. His power pales the moon." Turning away from his glow, she continued to walk. Elegguá watched as she did.

The fire burst into flames, and quickly he spread. Heat and smoke rose to the sky while everything he touched blackened and withered. "Look at me!" he screamed to the brightening sun and fading moon, "This is true power! I can destroy everything and my smoke blots out the sky in which you live!" It was true—thick, black smoke rose like curds to the sky, and quickly the world was thrust into a hazy twilight no matter how brightly the sun and moon tried to outshine each other. The air was hot, thick, and too acrid to breathe.

Elegguá shook his head sadly, and as fast as the wind he went running to the water. "Where are you going?" he called out.

"Away," said the water. "Their powers are great, indeed. Their ebós must have been greater than mine. I will never be as beautiful as the moon, or as bright as the sun, or as strong as the fire."

"Oh, but you will," said Elegguá. "For you are the only one who made ebó! The other three spirits lied." He wrapped the water in her black cloth and handed her the bag of machetes and knives. "And as the only one who made ebó, you are the only one who can put out the fire and save the world!"

Something happened to the water as she looked at Elegguá with confusion in her eyes; each element boasted of making ebó to seal in a powerful destiny, yet she made ebó just because Elegguá asked, and Elegguá said they lied. She spoke not a word and he offered no answers as her body wavered and spread over the earth; for the first time she felt and knew her power, as she was the great sea; she was all the rivers and lakes of the world. As she spread she lashed out at the fire; and the fire ran and climbed to higher ground while the sun laughed and the moon snickered at his fear. When her spirit filled the lowest parts of the watery world, still she spread and became the humidity in the air, the gentle vapor that rose to create white clouds. These darkened, and soon her black cloth unfolded until the earth found itself in twilight in which neither moon nor sun could be seen.

"Your power is greater than that of the fire, and it is greater than those of the sun and moon," Elegguá called out to her, "because you were the only one who made ebó!" Both spirits looked at each other fearfully as the water overpowered them in the sky. Her bag of machetes and knives ripped open from their weight and they fell to earth; and she, not wanting them to slice the creatures that crept on its face, reached out to grab them. She fell herself, first as gentle raindrops and then as powerful sheets of water drenching the earth. Over the fire she poured, and the fire, unable to burn through the water, died until he was but a few embers, and even these went out as they were soaked. "For making ebó," said Elegguá over the pounding rain, "your power has become the greatest in the world!"

The rain stood on the earth in shock; everywhere she looked there was water, some salty and some fresh, but most of the world was hers; and still, the sun and the moon were blotted out. "It doesn't matter what one's destiny is," said Elegguá, "because if ebó is not made, the blessings are never firm. Water owns this world; water saves this world; water will always be the most powerful thing in this world." Thus was the water's ashé sealed on the earth, and she was able to overcome the power of any element in the material realm.

The War between Fire and Water

From the Odu Irosun Meji (4-4)

Beneath all water and land the
fires still burn.

Fire and Water fought; the world trembled in fear; and the young woman over whose affections they dueled watched with morbid delight.

No one blamed them for their rivalry: her beauty was darkly seductive—her skin a deep, rich onyx, smooth like silk but softer. Her body curved gently, full where it was meant to be full and thin where it was meant to be thin. Childbearing hips swayed gently when she walked, like a slow metronome and hypnotic in their movement. Her breasts were round and full, bursting from her robes like two ripe melons—breasts meant for the suckling of children but perfect for the temptation of men. Her face was perfectly round with cheekbones so high they seemed unnatural; and her eyes were two pools of dark ink, dewy and reflective. She was the perfect woman, all things beautiful bound in one body of flesh. Had not the Fire and the Rain been warring for her love, the entire world of men might have fought for a chance with her; instead, the men and their families cowered fearfully, for day by day the war grew greater and more destructive.

What began as a competitive courtship grew into an argument, and soon, a fight; and even that grew until Fire and Water made the world their battleground. Tongues of flame rose up and licked the earth, scorching all it tasted; fire lashed out at the water, and blistering plumes of steam fought back. Water rose up with his full strength, emptying the oceans and the rivers and the seas until they were dry. The Fire burned and the Water splashed, and what was not reduced to ash became mush as water dampened the flames' fuel. When smoke obscured heaven's view of the earth, Olófin took notice. Angrily, he came down between the two elements using his body as a barrier between them and ordered, "Enough!"

Even the wet, charred mountains rumbled with the strength of his voice. Fire died down to a small flame while Water drew back into a single drop. They stood and looked at the destruction all around them, smoke and steam rising into a hazy sky. The woman hid her face shyly behind a feathered fan, only her eyes peeking through the thick peacock feathers. She giggled in spite of the destruction around her. Her name was Lust; and lust cared not who or what got hurt in her pursuit.

"This has to stop. It has to stop now!" Olófin ordered. The Fire wiggled nervously, and the Water rippled in shame; Lust giggled and walked away.

"But I love her," said the Fire. "And no one knows passion more than I."

"I love her," said the Water. "And no one knows the depth of emotion in the heart more than I."

Olófin sighed. "She loves neither of you, but Lust does what she was created to do—she enflames the heart with lust and toys with one's emotions. End this war now. Give me nine days to figure this out. At the end of this time I will know to whom this woman belongs."

Olófin left the two elements standing in face-off, but neither dared attack the other. Fire was the first to back down, and he went to see the diviners.

"I am in love," he said, his flames growing hotter as he thought about the woman. "And my enemy, Water, fights for her hand as well."

The old diviner frowned. "Water is not your enemy. Lust is the enemy that divides you both. Still, let us see what the orishas have to say." Carefully he cast the cowries on the mat. "If you want to win this war with Water you must make ebó: a goat to Elegguá, a bolt of white cloth, a bolt of black cloth, a bag of machetes, and plenty of money. Thus will you have the strength to win!"

Fire left the diviner's mat, his flames growing hotter as lust moved his loins. "Look at me!" he said to himself. "I am strong. I am powerful.

The Water cannot hold me back. I don't need to make ebó. I just need to wait for Olófin to make his decision. Lust is hot, like fire, and only Fire can be with her without being destroyed!"

Water made his way slowly to the diviner's house; when he got there, Fire was gone but the path was charred where he had walked. He knew he was the weaker of the two elements; but with lust in his heart, Water hoped there was a chance to win her hand. "I need help," he said.

"With what?" asked the diviner.

"Fire and I are in love with the same woman, and I am afraid she favors him over me. Olófin is trying to decide to whom the woman's hand and heart belong, but I want to make ebó to overcome the Fire."

Again, carefully the diviner cast his cowries. "To win this woman's heart you must make ebó: a goat to Elegguá, a bolt of white cloth, a bolt of black cloth, a bag of machetes, and plenty of money."

Water fed Elegguá gladly and gave him the cloth and machetes for which he asked. When his ebó was done, he emptied out his pockets and gave the diviner every penny he had. "Is this enough?" he asked the old man.

"It is more than enough," said the diviner.

That is when Olófin's call went out over the earth: "My decision is made. Water and Fire are to come to me, and I will give Lust's hand in marriage to one of the two."

Quickly, Fire and Water made their way to Olófin's palace.

Lust filled their hearts as they traveled; it fed Fire's flames, and as he ran through the world he burned and charred everything he touched. Water's heart was so full of lust that he thought he would burst; instead, he spread and grew as Elegguá unfolded the white cloth in the sky, and he became the white clouds floating lazily over the earth. Fire saw Water traveling in the sky, and he ran faster across the earth, growing larger and hotter, his smoke rising into the sky and blotting out even the white clouds. Water was angry, and his lustful anger made him darken; Elegguá spread the black cloth over the white, and soon Water was the angry storm, the dark clouds bursting over the earth in a downpour.

Fire tried to hide but with all the trees burnt and charred there was nowhere to hide; and with the earth wet and muddy, he could not withdraw to its center. Fire died that day in the rain, and Water was the only one to enter Olófin's palace.

He had no choice but to give Lust's hand and heart to Water, and so full of love and passion was he that he spread over the earth, refilling all the oceans and ponds and lakes and rivers. Because Water was the only one to make ebó, he became the most powerful and won the war for Lust's heart; and because lust itself is an overwhelming emotion, bringing destruction, even now there are times that the waters of the world rise up and overflow, bringing devastation and desolation with its floods.

Even the Fire comes back, enflamed with lust; but because the water made ebó and he did not, fire never wins. It always dies, and the water goes on forever.

The Cat, the Rat, and the Fish
From the Odu Irosun Odí (4-7)

Open your eyes and you will see there is
treason and danger everywhere.

The rat cowered in the reeds, soaked and cold but too afraid to move or even shiver; and his friend, the fish, sulked just below the river's surface enmeshed in weeds. From where they hid they saw the cat crouching on the other riverbank, flicking her tail as she sniffed at the damp earth. She was hungry; she was hunting; still, the scent of the rat and the fish evaded her twitching nose. Her movement was slow and methodical, and for what seemed hours the two friends hid hoping to avoid her.

Eventually the cat moved on to prey elsewhere. The rat peeked out from behind the weeds while the fish broke the surface. "That was close," whispered the rat.

"Too close," said the fish.

"She'll find us one day, you know." The rat shivered. His wet fur clung to his tiny body like glue, and the cool breeze blowing down the river chilled him. "And when she finds us, she will eat us!"

The fish shivered; ripples of water spread from his bullet-shaped body. He was used to the cold water, but fear made it seem colder; fear chilled him to his tiny bones. "I'm going to see the diviners," said the fish. "Desperate times call for desperate measures. I've watched too many of my friends and family fall into that cat's claws. I intend to survive."

"I'll go with you," said the rat. "We'll go together. Maybe the diviners can help both of us."

The rat scurried upstream toward the nearby city as the fish swam alongside him. The cat walked downstream so they knew they were safe—for a time. Where the riverbank ran beside the city, the rat hoisted the fish on his tiny back; and like this, the two scurried into town.

At Mofá's house the rat was exhausted and the fish on the verge of asphyxiation. Carefully, Mofá put the fish in a dish of water as the rat curled up protectively beside it. "You are a strange pair," said the old man. "And fish don't do well out of water. Something important must have brought you both here?"

"Yes," said the rat. The fish was still trying to catch his own breath in the bowl and could not speak for himself. "The cat hunts us every day. We are tired of hiding. We came to you for help."

"I see," said Mofá as he busied himself, preparing to divine for the fish and the rat. He thought, "Of all my clients, these two are the strangest pair."

The old man divined for the rat first. "The cat will eat you one day unless you make ebó," he told him. "To Elegguá offer a goat. To your head offer four pigeons. And to Obatalá offer a goat. Do these three things and you will live a long time on the earth."

He twitched his nose and whiskers nervously. "That is a large ebó," he said. "I am but a poor rat."

"How much is too much to save your own life?" He turned to the fish. "Now, fish, it is time to divine for you."

Carefully he set the bowl of water on the mat. The rat stood to the side hoping to watch. "Rat," Mofá said, "you have an ebó to prepare. I suggest you set off to prepare it now."

"I'm waiting for my friend," said the rat.

"Don't worry about your friend," said Mofá. "When we are done I will make sure he gets back to the river safely."

The rat refused to move; Mofá's eyes narrowed. "Rat, I dismissed you. Don't make me angry."

"Yes sir," he said, twitching his nose nervously again. Quickly, the rat scurried off.

"You, fish, have greater enemies than the cat. Know this: There are those who would take out their own eyes if it would make another blind. The rat is such a creature." On the mat Mofá divined; he prescribed the same ebós as he had the rat, but added, "After you finish your sacrifices we must wash you with okra and soap. Death is coming for you, fish, and this is the only way you will escape its claws."

Not wanting to die before his time, the fish made all the ebós Mofá marked. When they were done, the old man took him back to the river.

Rat never made his ebó.

Days later the rat scurried beside the riverbank looking for his friend, the fish. From time to time he stopped to nibble on some morsel he found in the weeds; and so lost was he in the moment that he forgot there was a cat prowling the riverside looking for prey. After hours of scavenging and scurrying, the rat all but bumped into the cat. He was running with his nose to the ground, sniffing for food when his head thumped into something soft and furry. He stood on his tiny hind legs and rubbed his head with his front feet, and when he looked up fear moved his bowels.

The cat was glaring and licking his teeth. A hungry growl rumbled in his stomach.

"What have we here?" asked the cat. His eyes narrowed. "Why, it's a little lost rat. Such a thin rat, but he looks tasty all the same." His mouth twitched as his diamond eyes thinned.

"I am thin," he stammered. "Too thin. Too thin to eat. Why, I'm all skin and bones." The rat held his tiny arms out to his side to show the cat how thin they were. "There's not much here to eat." Slowly he tried to back away.

The cat circled the rat, and the rat stood still. "Yes, your arms are thin. But look at your chest. Look at your haunches. They are thick. They will be good to eat."

"But I am old! And my meat is tough." He shook in fear, trying to find a way to escape the cat's stomach. Suddenly, he was sorry he refused to make ebó, and now was left to his wits to escape. "There are plenty of things to eat that are more tender and better tasting!"

"Really?" The cat sat back on his haunches. "What is there that would taste better than you? I see nothing else here but weeds and reeds."

"What about . . ." The rat turned two syllables into four, speaking slowly while his mind raced. "What about . . . a nice . . . tasty . . ." He strained, trying to think of something. "Fish! What about a nice tasty fish? I can show you where to get one!"

The cat's mouth watered. "Fish would be good. It is my favorite food. But look at the river, rat? Do you see any fish there? No. I've eaten most of them and now they hide from me. I'll eat you instead."

"Wait! The fish is my friend. He trusts me. I can call him and he will come. You can hide and when he breaks the water's surface you can catch him with your claws!" The rat felt no shame at his offer; he wanted to live no matter the cost, even if that meant betraying his friend.

The cat thought about this for a moment. "It's a deal," he said. "I will eat the fish instead of you." But the cat was not an honest creature, and he thought to himself, "After I eat the fish, I will eat you. Then I will be very full, indeed!"

Together they traveled further downstream, the cat crouching in the weeds just a few feet away from the river while the rat scurried alongside its bank. He called out for his friend, the fish, while the cat kept a careful eye on him. When the cat's stomach rumbled in hunger he almost lost his patience, but he crouched lower and stopped when he saw the fish break the water's surface.

"Rat!" he called out. "Where have you been? I made ebó with Mofá and he carried me back to the river. I've been looking for you for days! Did you make ebó so the cat won't eat you?"

"I did," said the rat. "I made ebó, and I'm safe from the cat. We have nothing to fear."

The cat heard not a word of this, so intent was he on the fish. Soundlessly he crept to the riverbank, still hiding behind the weeds and reeds as he stood at the water's edge.

"My ebó was a bit more complicated than yours, friend," said the fish. "For Mofá said there was treason and I had to wash myself with okra and soap. After my bath the most wonderful thing happened!"

The rat paid him no mind; the cat was within pouncing distance of him and the fish was still too far away. "I must bring him closer to me," he thought. "What did you say? I can't hear you, fish."

"What do you mean you can't hear me? I'm right here!" The fish swam closer.

"I don't know what's wrong with my ears today. I was walking too close to the river and I think I got water in them. Or something. Can you come closer and look for me?"

Fearlessly the fish swam to shore where the water was so shallow he had to push sand with his fins to move. When he and the rat were almost side by side, the cat pounced; his claws were open, and when the fish saw him flying through the air he tried to swim away but pushed futilely against the sand. The rat was fearless—the cat promised not to eat him—and he stood still.

Ten sharp claws tried to dig into the fish's flesh; the cat scooped him up, and rolled into the water. Yet the fish slipped through those claws as effortlessly as the water rolled off the cat's fur, for after he made his ebó his body grew thousands of tiny scales, each one as slimy as the okra and as slick as the soap, and no matter how hard the cat tried to hold him the fish slipped away.

When both the cat and the fish disappeared under the river, the rat smiled. The cat would have his prey and he would be safe. When the cat climbed out the river empty-handed and wet, the rat knew he had swallowed the fish whole and would be sated.

Instead, the cat scooped him up in his claws and held him tight. The rat could not move. Slowly the cat opened his mouth and dozens of razor sharp teeth hovered over the rat's head.

"Why?" he squealed. "I gave you my friend, the fish. You promised not to eat me!"

"Oh, I was always going to eat you," said the cat. His voice sounded sinister but smooth as he spoke. "I had no intention of keeping a promise to a traitor such as you. But the fish got away. His body was covered with a thick slime and I was unable to hold on to him with my claws. I tried to bite him, but he slipped right out of my mouth. So I'm very hungry, and I intend to eat you very slowly so I can enjoy each little bite."

Slowly did the cat feast on the rat, and as he promised, he enjoyed each tiny morsel. He began with the tail and worked up to his head, and the treasonous rat felt each bite. Worse, he knew that his friend the fish would not try to save him because he himself betrayed him.

That is what happens to those who do not make ebó: that is what happens to those who betray their friends. If the rat learned nothing else in his life, he learned that before he died.

5
PATAKÍS FROM THE COMPOSITES OF OCHÉ

Poverty and Hunger

From the Odu Oché Ejioko (5-2)

*There is no renewal without
decline.*

A buttery moon defied the darkness, its pale light casting shadows on the forest floor. The world slept, but through the trees three lonely figures walked with a single oil lamp lighting their way: Ikú, Poverty, and Hunger. Wordlessly they walked, the occasional snapping of a branch underfoot being their only sound. When they arrived at the roots of the ancient Iroko, Ikú placed the lamp firmly on the soft earth and the three made a tight circle around it. After a few moments of silence they spoke in hushed whispers.

"For years the two of you have wandered the earth without peace, without rest, and everywhere you go the humans rise up

71

against you. They force you to leave; and in loneliness, you keep moving. Are you not tired of it all?" asked Ikú. Her voice seemed filled with concern and sorrow; but in truth a creature such as she had little use for those emotions. She was as cold as the pale moon hanging over the earth.

"I am," said Hunger. "I find a town that seems peaceful and I try to settle but it's always the same. The humans fight me. I want nothing more than to rest and eat, to fill this hole that gnaws at my insides. But just when I start to feel full and sated they rise up and drive me from town. It has been like this since I can remember."

"And it's the same for me," said Poverty. "Everywhere I go, people work hard to banish me, and the more I fight to stay the more they work to get rid of me. All I want is a home, a place to call my own. But no one will let me settle. Maybe there is no room for poverty in this world?"

"Oh but there is!" Ikú clapped her hands together and smiled a huge, toothy grin as she spoke. "There is room for both of you in this world, but neither of you is strong enough to fight the humans alone. To succeed you must work together. Poverty, if you want a companion in life there is none more suited to be with you than Hunger; and, Hunger, if you want to remain in this world you must follow Poverty everywhere he goes. When people are poor they struggle to get rich. But when people are poor and hungry they have not the strength to fight. And once a village is impoverished and starving, all the osogbos of the world—sickness, disease, war, and even myself, death—all of us can live there as well, and no one can drive us away! Together the two of you can change the world and make it ours."

"What must we do?" Poverty asked, looking at Hunger. Hunger smiled back.

Ikú's voice was ethereal as she spoke, "This tree, this Iroko tree . . . it is the most ancient of its kind. Pacts are made here, vows that can never be broken. Swear together that the two of you will walk the world together and that you will never be apart. Do this and anyplace you settle will be yours. No one can separate you: no one can drive you away!"

Hunger and Poverty agreed; they placed their hands on the ancient Iroko and swore that they would walk the world together, never parting. Something shimmered in the night around them; a great power came from the ancient Iroko and sealed their fate.

Such was that power that even the orishas felt it in heaven. It worried them.

Hunger and Poverty walked out of the forest hand in hand. They felt much stronger together. The osogbos followed them, knowing that their strength would weaken the world and they would find power. The orishas in heaven looked down on the earth; they knew the world was changing, and soon it would be their time.

They watched, and waited.

Suffering doubled in the world that night.

Hand in hand Poverty and Hunger wandered the earth; and they traveled to towns they had already seen. "Let us go to Ilobú," said Poverty, remembering how inviting the town had seemed when he tried to settle there. "I went there once. I wanted to settle. But just as I made my home all the townspeople rose up and worked hard to drive me away. Oh . . . I so wanted to live there . . . it was such a wealthy town." His eyes were glazed and dreamy as he spoke to Hunger, and Hunger agreed to visit with his new friend.

Yet Hunger did not like what he saw. "The town of Ilobú is too small, my friend. I remember once a place called Oshogbo. It was thriving, sitting on the trade routes that ran from Ilé Ifé to Oyó. Anything a man wanted to eat could be found there, and I tried to eat it all. But those wretched humans drove me out when they felt my first pangs. I want to go back there."

Poverty agreed, and they wandered into Oshogbo. Everyone trembled when Poverty came; the town's coffers went dry and trade slowed to a standstill. For the first time, people felt *hunger*. Still, the town was small; the friends were unsatisfied, and Poverty had a thought. "There is a place known as Oyó. It is a burgeoning metropolis, a town whose inhabitants number in the thousands. There is wealth. There is an abundance of food. Let us go there!"

Little did they know that as they left, the osogbos came behind and besieged each town with their misfortunes. Hunger and Poverty walked the world, and in their wake they left death and destruction.

Obatalá came down from heaven followed by Shangó. They had seen enough. Slowly, they set about the job of cleaning up the mess Poverty and Hunger left in their wake. It was no easy job.

In ancient Oyó they found the city of their dreams: It was the heart of the Yoruba kingdom, the source of its unity and great wealth. The borders of Oyó sprawled before them, stretched out through the savannah like a leopard lazing by a river; its subjects numbered in the thousands, and their wealth was immeasurable. "I can live here," thought Poverty. "Such is the town's wealth that it will be moons before they know I have come, and then it will be too late."

Hunger licked his lips. Street vendors cooked every meat and vegetable imaginable; farms on the outskirts of town had an abundance of crops. His stomach rumbled. "I am starved, and there just might be enough food here for me to eat and feel sated!"

Hand in hand the two friends walked into Oyó; and when they disappeared into the crowds the osogbos gathered outside the city gates. Ikú was at the forefront. "Soon . . ." said Ikú to her siblings. "Soon Oyó will succumb to poverty and hunger, and when it does the ancient city will be ours to destroy."

By nightfall the city's woeful cries began. Merchants were unable to move their wares, and fathers came home to empty tables and hungry children. In shadows the misfortunes slipped through city walls and invaded homes. Sickness, arguments, wars, and death came to Oyó that day.

Obatalá came as well. He stood outside the city gates and watched.

"This cannot be allowed to continue," he said to himself. Quietly so no one could hear he slipped into town. By morning he found the two friends.

He stood before Poverty and Hunger, his aged body shaking and trembling in mortal form. Still, he held a single hand up and with a voice as pure and strong as the ashé of heaven commanded, "Stop!"

Poverty and Hunger giggled before him, for behind them stood all the misfortunes of creation. "You have no power here, old man," said Poverty. "We stand on the shoulders of all the osogbos in the world. Our ashé here is great. Go back to heaven where you belong."

"Yes," said Hunger. "The mortal core is weak where we stand. And behind us all the misfortunes of the world follow. Human eyes turn away from heaven when they are poor and hungry. And without eyes to see the light, can there be anything but darkness?"

Fifteen osogbos encircled Obatalá as Ikú moved to stand between Poverty and Hunger. "Between poverty and hunger there can be only death. They bring darkness and desperation; they weaken the human will and it succumbs to evil. What can you do to us now, old man?"

Obatalá stiffened before Poverty and Hunger; he felt his mortal form grow heavy as they were near, but still he found the strength to gesture to heaven. "I can make ebó. I can gather all the spirits of heaven behind my back as Poverty and Hunger gather the osogbos behind theirs. But more importantly, I can bring hope to the world."

Obatalá glowed with a preternatural light, a soft but warm glow that pushed back the osogbos. He was light; Ikú was darkness, and soon Poverty and Hunger stood alone, trembling together as Obatalá's form seemed to tower above them. "You cannot separate us, old man. We made a pact at the feet of the Iroko."

Obatalá crossed his hands over his chest and looked beyond the light to see the osogbos cowering among the shadows of the trees. There was a white-hot fire in his eyes, and in fear they fled. Still, Poverty and Hunger stood firm before him; they shook, but they stood their ground. "It is true that pacts cannot be broken, but foolish pacts have a way of recoiling against those who make them." Greater grew the light; Poverty and Hunger sank to their knees. Still, they clutched each other. "Your pact will be honored by heaven; as King of all the orishas I speak on that with heaven's authority. Together you will wander the world hand in hand; and you will have the power, together, to settle where you will. Osogbo will follow you everywhere you go, as such was the design of Ikú when he led you to make your pact."

Poverty and Hunger smiled—they knew their pact was strong, unbreakable. But Obatalá continued, and his words turned their smiles to frightened frowns. "There is no renewal in this world without decline. You will bring suffering, but the very suffering you bring will be your own undoing. For when humans have suffered enough, when their lives are so tragic and so unbearable that they cannot go on, they will turn to us, the orishas. They will turn their eyes away from you and come to our diviners; and they will make ebó; and as they make ebó we ourselves will intercede from heaven and drive away the very osogbos you bring with you, just as I have driven them away today. And when they are gone you will be all that is left, and you will be forced into submission. You will tremble and grovel then as you are now, and if you hope to live you will have to flee. For we will bless our own with abundance; we will feed our own with our own hands, and where there is abundance and plenty, there can be no poverty and hunger."

Heaven's light blinded their eyes; backward they crawled as the pure light of heaven burned and stung their skin. Obatalá smiled. "You will take your evil to new places—where you walk osogbo will follow. But know that behind them we follow, and you will be forced to wander and flee all your lives."

Osogbo fled that day, and Poverty and Hunger were powerless to remain as ashé flowed from heaven to the earth. Since then they have wandered the world, together; and every place they sought to settle, when humans felt they suffered enough they went to the diviners and made ebó. Instead of destroying the world with their pact, they renewed it.

The Birth of Menstruation
From the Odu Oché Irosun (5-4)

*The man with a hole in his sack does not
know he is being followed.*

A silent arrow sliced the air, sailing a straight line to the deer's heart. Its hind legs buckled and it fell tail first to the earth before rolling on its side, dead. Its legs were still kicking when the hunter ran to it; even in death it tried to escape. When it lay silent and unmoving, the hunter let out a great cry, his powerful arms holding the bow above his head in triumph.

Blood trickled from where the arrow pierced the animal's body.

He hoisted it on his back and walked deeper into the forest, dropping it gently at the roots of an ancient Iroko tree. With a sharp knife and a few minutes' work he sawed off the deer's head, and blood gushed from the neck's stump. He laid the head among the roots and waited for the lights to come, the soft, gentle orbs that traveled down the tree's trunk bringing Olófin's spirit with them. They were subtle at first, those orbs, faint balls of light barely visible; and something almost transparent rose from the blood as they came. It was a soft shimmer against the dark wood of the tree like heat rising in the desert, and it disappeared into the orbs. When they faded an old man stood in their place; in his hands was the deer's head.

The pact was sealed. Olófin blessed the hunter silently before fading; and the hunter, having renewed his pact with the ancient orisha, returned home with the carcass. His pact was simple—he fed Olófin and he, in return, gave him the ashé to hunt so he could feed his family.

The hunter's wife was a curious woman; she wondered about the headless animals he brought home. One night her curiosity got the best of her and she filled his hunting sack with ashes, cutting a tiny hole in the bag's bottom. When he left for the forest in the morning, the ashes would leave a trail and she could follow him at a distance wherever he went; thus would she learn the mystery.

The next day, after her husband arose early and left for the hunt, the curious wife followed the ashes at a distance, silently. It was not long before he had tracked game. A swift arrow found its mark and the animal found death. The hunter gathered the carcass and went to the Iroko tree, and there he let the blood fall onto the earth. Once the head was in its roots, Olófin came for the offering and asked, "My son, why have you allowed another to follow you to this sacred place?"

Olófin pointed to a thick grove of trees, and the hunter turned to see his wife standing among them, her mouth open in a gesture of disbelief for having been discovered. "Woman," said Olófin, "blood you wished to see, and blood you shall ever shed to honor me!" Because of the wife's curiosity and Olófin's decree, women from that day have shed their own blood every month. It was a pact born of one woman's curiosity, and since that time women have shielded themselves from men as they bled from the womb.

How the Hummingbird Was Born
From the Odu Oché Meji

All things change for love; the world will
not remain always as it is.

She was young, and she was beautiful; and her heart was light as she sat by the river, her feet dangling among budding lilies. Her hands caressed the polished river pebble that hung on a silver chain at her throat; it was a gift from the man who loved her, and she loved it more than anything she owned.

"I will be wed soon," she whispered to the slow-moving water, she who was the princess known as Odedei. "I am in love, and he loves me, and tonight we will announce our love to my father and he will be happy to see me wed." A light breeze rippled the river's surface; the lilies and reeds seemed to bounce with silent laughter, like that of young girls sharing an innocent secret. "When I come again you will bloom," she said to the lily buds floating above their green pads, "as will my heart, because I will be a married woman."

Gently she stood, taking her slippers in her hands, and her walk was almost a skip as she made her way home. Odede, her suitor, would meet her there; and after asking her father's permission to wed, on bended knee he would ask her to be his wife. It was how they planned it.

Even the best-laid plans go to wrong.

It took many days of travel, but Ocanancan made the journey to Odedei's palace. He came with many men and dozens of horses and bags of gold and jewels and trinkets as presents for her father, the King. It was the King's servant, Odede, who met the weary caravan; and without so much as a nod to the young man, Ocanancan jumped off his horse and made his way inside. As was his duty, Odede showed the rich merchant's men where to tie their horses; and once they were secure, together they brought the bags into the King's palace.

Ocanancan gestured to the bags as Odede and his own servants brought them inside the palace. "This, kind sir, is what I offer you for your daughter's hand in marriage."

Odede froze; his heart leapt in his throat and settled there like cold ice cubes.

One by one the men approached the King, carefully opening their bags so he could see the riches inside. Odede moved slowly, his legs wobbly and weak. He was the last to approach the King. He saw the wealth inside his one bag, more than he would make in a lifetime of servitude to his master. He fought back the bitter tears that stung his eyes, and forced an uneven smile.

The King barely noticed.

"She is my youngest," he said. "And my favorite," he added. The

King grew silent. Ocanancan held his breath. "Do you promise to be kind to her?"

"I do," he said, his head bowed with his right fist over his heart.

"Do you promise to love her and keep her as is fit a King's daughter?"

"I love her already, and I have more than enough wealth to offer her the finest things."

He walked to Ocanancan and embraced him roughly; he was startled at first, and settled into the King's embrace just in time for him to break it. "Welcome to the family . . . son."

Odede thought he would faint.

Odedei saw the horses tied outside her home; she eyed them curiously before bursting inside. "Father?" she called out, her voiced echoing off the palace walls. She ran through halls and stopped when she saw dozens of men gathered inside the King's throne room, and her one true love, Odede, standing still with a heavy bag in his hands. It was open; she thought she saw the glint of gold. The men parted slowly, a great sigh erupting in the hall when they saw the beautiful maiden standing before them. She breathed heavily, her ample chest rising and falling with each breath. She saw the old merchant standing before her father as he sat in his great throne, and she wrinkled her brow when the stranger came to her and got down on one knee.

"Odedei," he said, taking her hands in his. She was too surprised to pull back, and her glance flew from her father's smiling face to the forlorn look of her lover, Odede. His eyes were reddened as if he were about to cry or scream in anger—she could not tell which. "Your beauty is legendary as is your heart. I have traveled a great distance to bring gold and jewels and trinkets to your father, the King. I have come a long way to ask his permission to marry you, and now that I have his permission I ask you . . . will you be my wife?"

There was a great clattering of metal on the stone floor; Odede had dropped the bag he was holding, and gold coins rolled on the hard floor. The glint of gold sparkled and shimmered in the evening light that came through open windows; all eyes were on him as he said, "I'm sorry. I can't . . ." and he ran from the room with a heavy heart.

Odedei's eyes welled with angry tears as she saw the small fortune of gold rolling out on the floor; she breathed in sharply as Odede walked briskly from the room, and her stomach lurched as she saw her father smiling at the small fortune laying on the floor like a child's discarded toys. Her eyes took in the bags the dozens of men held; they bulged, and she knew each bulged with a small fortune. "You came here to buy me?" It was an accusation, not a question. She looked at her father with tearful eyes. "And you sold me?"

"It's not like that," said Ocanancan. Still holding her hands he stood and looked at her tear-swollen face. "I love you."

"Love can't be bought. I hate you! I am in love with another."

The men gasped as she ran from the room; she ran up the stairs to her own chambers and slammed the door, hard. The palace walls shook with her anger as she screamed. Then there was only silence.

"She'll come around," said the King.

It did not take long for her father to plan her wedding.

Odedei loved the full moon; on nights when it hung low and full in the sky, she spent hours walking on the riverbank, following its reflection in the water. "This," her father told her, "the night of the full moon will be your wedding night." She sat by him unmoving as he went through the plans in his head. "It will be beautiful. We will wait for the moon to rise; and the courtyard will be lit by hundreds of flaming torches. There, by moonlight and torchlight you and Ocanancan will make your vows to each other, and the priests will bless your union."

"I will die before I marry that man," she said, barely a whisper.

"What?"

Louder she said, "I will die before I marry that man. The dark moon is in less than two weeks. When the moon is dark, I will kill myself."

It was true that the King loved his daughter, but his love of wealth was even greater. "You cannot mean that!" he said. "Ocanancan is a wealthy man who could have anyone he wanted. Anyone. And he chose you. It is a great honor, young lady."

"Honor be damned!" she screamed. "I have loved Odede since the day I first saw him. The day that man *bought* me from you, we were going to announce our love, and he was going to ask your permission to marry me."

"My servant?" The King laughed. "My *servant* thought he was good enough for my daughter? You would choose a life of poverty over a life of wealth and comfort?"

"I would choose a single day of love over eternal life without it," she said.

"You will marry Ocanancan, daughter." It was a warning, not a command. "You will marry him or you won't have to worry about taking your own life. I will lock you in my prison before I let you marry Odede."

She stormed away from her father in tears. A life without love was no better than death; and if she had to die, she would do it in the river, with the lilies she loved. "They should be blooming now," she thought to herself. "And they will find my bloated body floating among their blossoms."

Odedei was unable to carry out her plans.

Her father, the King, set a guard outside her door day and night; and she was kept prisoner in her own room. A handmaiden came throughout the day to bring her meals, but Odedei did not eat—her heart was broken, and nothing works inside the body of a woman with a broken heart, not even her stomach. She spent her days beside her window looking over the courtyard, and she would have thrown herself to the ground below had the window not been nailed shut. Night after night she lay in her bed watching the moon rise over the horizon; she counted the days until it would be full.

"My father keeps me prisoner until I am married," she whispered to the moon. "I would sooner kill myself than be married to that man. If I were free, I would run to the river and throw my body into it. I would sink to its bottom and breathe in deeply of its water." She sighed. "But I can no more get to the river than I can get out of this room."

That night, the night before her wedding, the moon hung low and almost full in the dark sky. She cried like a prisoner about to go to the gallows when her handmaiden crept quietly into the room. "Why do you cry?" she asked. "Tomorrow you will be wed to the richest man in the land, a man with more wealth than your own father. Are you not happy?"

"I am not," she said, burying her face in her hands. "I do not love Ocanancan. I am in love with Odede."

"You will learn to love him?"

"I won't."

"But you will. He has a kind heart."

"He's not that kind," she seethed. "It is because of him and his money that I am kept locked up in my room, a prisoner. If I were a free woman I'd throw myself to the river."

The handmaiden gasped. "Mistress, do not speak like that. It frightens me. What can I do to soothe you?"

"You can set me free."

"That I cannot do."

Odedei thought silently for a moment. She looked out her window and up at the moon. It was sailing higher in the sky, beyond the reach of her window. She had a thought. "You can do something for me that will soothe me," she said.

"Anything—I will do anything for you."

Odedei reached around the back of her neck and unclasped the chain that held a polished river stone against her neck. "Take this to Odede," she said.

"Your necklace? But it is your favorite in the entire world."

"Yes," she sighed. "It is my favorite in the entire world because he gave it to me. He took a small amber stone from the riverbank and set it in silver; and then he bound it to this silver chain. He gave it to me in the place where the water lilies grow. It was there that he told me he loved me. It was there that I said I loved him. And it was there that we kissed for the first time." She held out the pendant to her servant, and carefully she took it from her. She tucked Odedei's charm in her pockets. "Tell him this: tell him that even though I am forced to marry Ocanancan tomorrow night with the rising of the full moon, he is the man that I love. Tell him that my heart will die when I take my vows, and I will die not long after. I will be as one of the dead among the waters and the lilies that grow in our special place. Tell him . . . after my wedding ceremony he is to throw that stone into the river; that is where our love was born, and that is where my heart will die."

Her words made the handmaiden shiver, but she had promised to do her mistress' bidding. She kissed her lightly on the cheek and the two women embraced. "I will go to him now." She turned to leave, and as she stepped through the door she stopped and turned. "Ocanancan is a good man. Even if you do not love him, he loves you. He will take good care of you."

It was the night of her wedding and as her father promised the court-yard was ablaze with torches and candles. It seemed the entire kingdom was there to watch the ceremony, the night Odedei was to become Ocanancan's wife.

For the first time she was freed from her room. She sat in her father's parlor surrounded by handmaidens who dressed her and coiffed her hair. When they were done they stood back to look—she was beautiful, a black lotus rising from white cloth. There were no words; the room was silent.

"Leave me now," ordered Odedei.

"But we can't," protested her handmaiden. "Your father said to keep watch over you until the wedding."

"So you stand guard outside the door." Her chest rose and fell in anger, her breasts all but bursting from their cloth. "What do you think I will do? Jump out of the window? Now go!"

One by one the women backed out the door, each casting a wary eye at her and then each other. When the last handmaiden left she shut the door, and Odedei did just what she told them she would not do—she jumped out the window.

She was, after all, on the first floor.

With the light of the full moon guiding her steps she ran, her white wedding dress trailing behind her and ripping in the undergrowth. When she got to the river where the water lilies and lotuses grew she stopped, breathless; there before her was her lover, Odede.

There was only one thing they could do—they embraced, and kissed. The night seemed on fire with their passion.

"How did you get away?" Odede asked.

"I jumped!" she said, a wry smile on her face.

"Then those torches bouncing through the forest toward us must be for you." Odedei looked behind her; the forest seemed on fire with their light. There were hundreds of them marching slowly toward the river, and soon she heard her name being called out. "They will find us both," Odede said.

"Oshún, save us!" she cried to the river. There was no answer; there was only the sound of the river bubbling away in the night. "Oshún, you must save us, or I will die in your depths." With those words she broke away from Odede and threw herself into the water. He panicked, and jumped in after her.

As she exhaled and was about to take in her first mouthful of water, Oshún did, indeed, have pity on the two lovers. She turned them both into hummingbirds, and while the townspeople scoured the woods looking for them both, they flitted among the lotuses that grew under the light of the full moon.

And that is how the hummingbird was born.

Even a Woman Can Hunt

From the Odu Oché Ejila (5-12)

Remember and respect your mother—of
all the women in the world, there is no
woman more powerful than she.

The village hunters told her, "No woman should use a knife to kill; it will destroy you and make you sick." But she and her children were hungry, and the hunters would not feed them unless she had sex with them. She had no use for men or sex in her life now; she only wanted to feed her children. And it was for this reason that she stood alone in the forest, afraid, but determined to hunt.

The air was hot and sticky. Salty sweat stung her eyes, and she lifted an arm thickly swathed with cloth to wipe her brow. In her free hand she clutched a knife; her knuckles were ashen, she held it so tightly.

Her stomach rumbled; she trembled, weakened with hunger and overcome with fear. Yet she knew they were as hungry as she. Gathering her strength, she rustled and shook the low-hanging tree branches. She kicked at the twigs and leaves making noise; it wasn't a lot of noise, but she knew it was enough to attract the leopard.

And it was.

Silently it stalked her as she stumbled through the underbrush; but she knew it was there. She got quiet and braced herself for its attack. It came at her, a snarling, hungry beast flying through the air.

By instinct, without thought, she lifted her left forearm and felt powerful jaws clamping down. The thick cloth protected her arm, but not entirely, and she felt sharp teeth grazing her skin. The leopard twisted her to the ground, and bit harder, but she brought her knife up and into its soft chest, twisting it hard as she herself let out a primal scream. She heard ripping flesh, and the sickening sound of metal scraping bone. Hot blood sprayed her face.

The jaw went slack, and the leopard lay on top of her, dead.

It took all of her strength, but she rolled the animal off herself; and she stood, shaking. Carefully she unwound the cloth from her forearm and saw that the teeth barely punctured her skin, and she smiled. She hummed as she skinned the beast, and let the innards slip from its flesh. Carefully, she packed the fresh meat into the leopard skin and carried it home, to her children.

Oshún felt strong, powerful; and she smiled, for even without a man, her children would eat well tonight.

6

PATAKÍS FROM THE COMPOSITES OF OBARA

The Mountain
From the Odu Obara Ogundá (6-3)

The mountain believed itself to
be powerful and did not make
ebó; thus did it fall.

Beneath the cold, salty sea the mountain stood; it was rooted in its depths, poking through the upper waves. When Obatalá came down on the golden chain to separate water and earth, the mountain was the first to rise, his gentle water-worn slopes and rounded top no longer brushing the waves. He touched heaven. He was the crown of all creation, or so he thought.

The mountain believed itself to be powerful.

One by one the animals came, each offering a sacrifice to survive in the new world. Obatalá molded humans by the sea, and the mountain watched; he was there when they opened their eyes on the rolling, churning surf; and when they turned their faces to the mountain and saw the sun shining down on them through its peaks and slopes, they fell prostrate on the earth and worshipped all of heaven. The orishas taught them all they knew about the world, but more importantly, they taught the humans how to worship and make ebó. Soon the elements of creation did the same—they made ebó and fought for supremacy in the material world. The wind, the rain, the ocean, the sun, the moon, the stars, the air, and the earth—all these made offerings to the orishas hoping to increase their lot in life. All, that is, except for the mountain.

The mountain believed itself to be powerful and did not make ebó.

As the years passed the sea rose up and sank back, eating at the mountain's foundation; so angry was she that he rose free of her grip that she tried, bit by bit, to bring him down. The mountain was unafraid. The earth was jealous; she stood in his shadow and hated how everyone looked up at the mountain and down on her. Slowly she shifted beneath his weight hoping to bring him down; tiny cracks opening deep in the earth. The mountain was unmoved. The sun was angry that people looked at the mountain lovingly, but turned their eyes away and hid from him in the mountain's shadows; and the moon was jealous that he reached so high as to brush her stars. With his heat the sun baked the mountain's surface, and at night the moon sent falling stars to crash in his face. The wind, the rain, the storm, and the lightning—they, too, took offense at the mountain's arrogance and they did what they could to erode its surface. The mountain barely noticed.

"You cannot hurt me, not any of you!" he called out. "For I am the greatest in the world—I am stronger than any one of you!"

Such did he anger them that they all, at the same time, doubled their efforts. The earth shook in anger, all her cracks coming together and creating a huge crevice that yawned out to sea; and the water rose up as the earth rumbled and shook, sending a great typhoon crashing into the mountain. The sun bore down with all its might, and the winds and the rains gathered into a storm so angry that the world trembled in fear. It all happened quickly, and in a matter of minutes the mountain crumbled, its cries of anger shaking to the very foundation of heaven. When the world again grew quiet, the mountain was no more.

For the mountain believed it was powerful and did not make ebó; thus did it fall.

Money Is Trouble, and Trouble Is Death
From the Odu Obara Irosun (6-4)

Money is an evil mistress, and those who lust for her find death as their reward.

She lay lifeless in the road, a black ragdoll dressed in the finest silk robes. Her limbs hung at unnatural angles to her body and her eyes were open full-stare, the white clouds and sunlight reflected in her inky black pupils. When Obatalá and his three brothers stumbled upon her they thought she might be alive; the younger brother thought he saw the rising and falling of her chest. It was only the afternoon breeze skirting across the forest floor, rippling the fabric hanging loosely across her breasts. Obatalá kept walking while the three brothers encircled her, staring at her hair. It was almost as long as she was tall, and it was strung with thousands upon thousands of cowries. Cowries were wealth, and it was all wasted in the hair of a corpse.

There on the road between Obatalá's two kingdoms, Iranje Ilé and Iranje Oko, they found a corpse, and she was beautiful.

Obatalá slowed his pace. Without looking over his shoulder he called out to his brothers, "That is Ajé, Olokun's daughter. Let her be and keep walking."

The oldest brother looked up and called out to Obatalá, "But she's dead. We have to do something."

The other two brothers kept staring at her hair.

"Neither wait on her nor watch her. Ajé is the beginning of trouble." He kept walking, and soon was out of sight.

"Why won't Obatalá wait for us? Why isn't he concerned about this woman?" He gazed at her face. "This beautiful woman," he added.

"How long do you think she has been here?" asked the middle brother.

"Not long," said the oldest. "She still looks . . . alive."

They stared at her hair. Finally the oldest said, "There must be thousands of cowries woven in her hair."

"More," said the youngest. "Each strand is as tall as she, and there are hundreds upon hundreds of tiny braids in her hair. She was a rich woman."

The middle brother knelt beside her and caressed her face. Her skin was still warm, not cold; it was as if she was still alive with blood pumping in her veins. He trembled. Her beauty was overwhelming, and the riches she had in her hair were obscene. Taking a knife from his shoulder bag, carefully and with shaking hands, he cut off a single braid. The two brothers, still standing, gasped.

He slipped the cowries off the tiny braid; there were hundreds on that one strand. "Take this, brother," he said giving them to the youngest. "Go back to town and buy us food. We will move the body from the road. And we will figure out what to do with her."

It was only a quarter day's walk back to Iranje Ilé, but it was already afternoon. "I won't be back until well after sunset."

"We'll be fine," said the middle brother. Quickly, the youngest ran back to town. Already there was treason in his heart.

When the youngest disappeared past a bend in the road, the eldest turned to the middle brother. "He has always been a burden, a drain on our resources."

"Yes," said the middle brother. "But now the three of us are rich.

Obatalá is gone and there is no one to see us take the cowries from her hair."

"True. The three of us will be rich. But if the riches were split two ways, we'd be very comfortable for a long, long time." The oldest brother's eyes were glazed; they looked feverish, and the other brother watched as the whites slowly reddened. Again the eldest knelt and touched Ajé's face. He caressed her and looked at her hair. "All that wealth."

"Brother, what is wrong with you? You touch the corpse like a man touches his wife."

He didn't answer; instead, he ran his fingers through her braids. The cowries clicked gently as he disturbed them. "Her skin is so soft, so warm; and her hair so thick. Isn't she beautiful?" There was madness in his voice when he said again, "Touch her. Just touch her."

Trembling, the middle brother did the same. He felt the warmth of her skin, and the same fever that burned in his brother was stoked in him. "I feel it. And all this wealth." His voice trailed off; it was soft and dreamy when he said, "We can kill our younger brother and have all this for ourselves. Why should we share such a beautiful woman with him?"

They spent the rest of the afternoon and evening stroking Ajé's lifeless body, speaking in hushed whispers of how they planned to murder their brother. And secretly, they plotted how to kill each other.

They forgot about Obatalá.

In town the youngest bought food; but there was fire in his heart and beneath his skin when he thought of the lifeless woman lying in the road. "Ajé," he whispered to himself again and again, almost a chant. His heart settled on her name and it became his mantra, his focus. "Ajé," he said a bit louder.

"What was that?" asked the street vendor. He saw madness in the young man's eyes. Watching him carefully he wrapped the food in cornhusks and watched as he put them in his travel bag.

"Nothing," he said handing him the cowries. He was about to walk away when he stopped; he turned, and looked at the street vendor. The vendor shivered under his gaze. "We have rats at home. I need to kill them. Where can I buy poison?"

Trembling, wanting to be rid of the young man, he pointed at a shop across the street. "There!" It was a command—he wanted to be rid of the stranger.

"Thank you." He smiled, but it was a wicked grin. As he disappeared into the shop the street vendor sighed and closed his eyes. He was afraid—he had seen the mask of evil, a mask worn on the face of that young man.

He hoped to never see him again.

The youngest returned to the road as quickly as he could; night fell, but the cold, pale moonlight lit the path well. He found his older brothers sitting beside the woman's corpse; they had built a small fire. He was glad, for the fever that burned his skin brought chill and he sat by the fire to warm himself.

"You're late," said the oldest.

"Very late," said the middle brother.

"Not too late," said the youngest. "It was a long journey."

"Where is our food?" asked the oldest.

"And our change," said the middle brother. "It's not all yours. It is meant to be split three ways."

As the youngest brother set the cornhusk-wrapped food by the fire and the cowries beside that, the older brother picked up a branch from the fire. One end was red-hot and the other still cool. "What are you doing?" the youngest asked.

"We can use that to warm the food," said the middle brother.

The eldest laughed; and his laughter was warped, pained. It was the laughter of a thousand maniacs, and both brothers shivered. "Or, we can use it to kill you!"

"Yeah, right," the youngest said, getting to his feet.

Both brothers jumped on him then; they beat him with the red-hot stick and their fists. They smashed his head in the rocks encircling the fire, and kicked him in his ribs. When they were done there was blood and gore; the youngest brother's eyes went gray and his face ashen. In death, his corpse looked like a corpse, a stark contrast to Ajé, whose body was lifeless but beautiful.

The middle brother picked up a cornhusk and unwrapped the tamale inside; he took a bite, and handed another to his brother. "Delicious," he said.

With his own mouth full, the eldest mumbled, "You know when I'm done with this tamale I'm going to kill you, too."

"You won't," said the middle brother. "Because I'm going to kill you first."

They ate in silence, each watching the other warily. The poison took hold slowly; it was like falling asleep, and each fought it as long as they could. On either side of Ajé they collapsed, and when their eyes were gray and their bodies silent, Ajé stood up.

She walked away into the forest, leaving the three bodies by the fire.

Obatalá was in Iranje Oko for eight days; when his business was done there, he returned to Iranje Ilé. On his journey between the two towns he came upon the bodies of the three brothers; they lay beside a fire that had long ago grown cold. Ajé was nowhere to be seen.

"Money is such an evil mistress," he whispered.

He touched each corpse with his staff; slowly, the sores and rot that ate their flesh healed, and color returned to their skin. "Arise!" he ordered, and one by one the bodies rose from the earth stiffly. Their eyes lost their gray, and with a great gasp each corpse took a breath. Their movements were stiff, but move they did; they stretched, and reached, and stood.

"What happened here?" It was a command, not a question; and each brother told their story.

When they were done Obatalá said, "Did I not warn you to leave Ajé alone? Lust for money leads to death; and death is an evil creature.

She cares not who she kills—she only wants to kill. Like you three, all who love money will not live long. They will always want more; they will never be satisfied, and their lust for riches will lead to trouble and death. One must have patience and wisdom in the pursuit of money."

"We have learned our lesson," said the eldest brother. "Never again will we be greedy; we will always seek wisdom before we seek wealth that we do not deserve."

"You have learned well, but you have learned too late." Obatalá walked away from the three brothers sadly; they remained standing by the cold fire pit. When Obatalá was gone, the coldness of death returned, and one by one each brother fell down, dead.

Since then the lust for wealth has been an evil thing, and those who succumb to their lust find death as their reward. Wealth is an evil mistress with no loyalty; and she remains in this world while those who love her too fiercely move on to the next.

How the Rosary Bead Plant Got Its Ashé

From the Odu Obara Odí (6-7)

The peony seed could not decide whether
it was red or whether it was black, but it
was still just a single seed all the same.

The earth stood still the day Olófin walked on its face. Eshu walked with him. The old man had not come to visit; he came to create, and he called Eshu to witness the work he was about to do. From the folds of his robe he pulled two beads, one red and one black. They rested on his left palm, and he held them close to his eyes. Olófin looked at them and whispered, "Things in this world are not always as they seem. Would it not be nice to have a plant that held that truth?"

Eshu stood beside him; he watched Olófin as he stared at the two tiny beads. "Sometimes, Father, when I walk, people on one side of me see red while those on the other see only black." Olófin looked up and smiled at Eshu. "Entire kingdoms have fallen from just that."

"Yes," said Olófin, "you are a very tricky orisha, Eshu. Perhaps you should consider letting your colors mingle into a pattern. Half red on one side and half black on the other can be . . . confusing. It causes too much trouble."

"Is that not what I'm meant to do?" Eshu smiled, and Olófin smiled back. It was exactly what he was meant to do.

Olófin's gaze returned to the two beads and he sighed, his breath rolling the beads around in his palm until they stuck together and became one. "Something so insignificant, the color of your dress, can cause so much heartache."

"Look at your bead, Olófin. It cannot decide whether it is red or whether it is black. It is like me!"

"It holds both in potential, Eshu, and that, as with you, is what will make this new plant so powerful." Stiffly he bent to the earth and pushed the red and black bead in the soil. He whispered a few words to the earth. Eshu strained to hear but Olófin's voice was too soft. Some words were meant only for the ears of God.

As if by magic a vine sprouted from the earth; and this grew into a bush. Thousands of red and black seeds hung in its branches.

"This, Eshu, is my special plant—'Iwereyeye' is its name. Of all the plants in the world, only this was made by my hands. It will be elder to all the other plants in the world, and its ashé is great."

Eshu smiled; each bead was dressed as well as he, black on one side and red on the other. "This," mumbled Eshu, "is sure to bring trouble to the world."

"Or great evolution." Olófin smiled. His ears were old, but no sound escaped them, not even Eshu's whispers.

In those days Obatalá was establishing himself on earth as a great king; and wanting to keep his head straight and focused, he called for Olófin and asked him to bless his orí. Olófin came; he came with handfuls of Iwereyeye to bless Obatalá's head.

"I cannot use that plant to make ebó," said Obatalá, incredulous that Olófin would recommend such a thing. "I am an orisha of but a single word, and that plant is like Eshu—wild and indecisive. The seeds cannot decide if they want to be red, or if they want to be black."

"But I made that plant with Eshu as my witness. It embodies the nature of this world—that it is, indeed, indecisive and wild. If you want your head to rise above all others you must make ebó with it. Wash your head with its leaves, and nothing can ever sway your mind."

"Nothing sways me now. Certainly, I won't be swayed to use this on my head!" He lifted his cane and pointed it at the plant. "It has no ashé for me."

Olófin sighed. Obatalá might be an orisha of great wisdom, but he was also an orisha of great stubbornness. "So be it," said Olófin. "Serve your own head as you wish." With those words he melted from Obatalá's sight.

Obatalá called his priests to serve his head with white, cool things. "This," he thought, "is how one must sustain orí."

The days turned to weeks, and the weeks turned to months, and the months rolled out into years; Obatalá ruled with a heavy but fair hand as the world laid its problems at his feet. One day he sat idly in his chambers staring out the window, watching white clouds roll by in an azure sky. When a richly dressed man entered his room he jumped, startled. As his heart pounded in his chest he stared at the young man; his clothes were red and white, and cowries were sewn into its hems. "This is a rich man," Obatalá thought.

"I'm sorry if I startled you, Father," said the young man as he stretched out in obeisance on the floor. He waited for Obatalá to bless him; instead, Obatalá stood there staring.

"Father? You called me Father. Who are you?"

"Are you kidding me?" Shangó looked up from where he lay.

"No. Who are you?"

Shangó drew himself into a sitting position on the floor and looked at Obatalá. His eyes were vacant, his head tilted to the side. The old man shook where he stood. "Obatalá—it's me, Shangó."

The fog cleared from the orisha's eyes, and his mouth fell open with surprise. "Shangó! My son! When did you get here?"

With narrowed eyes Shangó stretched out on the floor before him; fingers brushed the young one's shoulders lightly as Obatalá offered his blessing. Shangó stood, and the two men embraced. "It is good to see you, Shangó. It has been too long."

"But I was just here this morning," Shangó thought.

Soon the other orishas noticed something was wrong with Obatalá; at random moments his eyes would go vacant, and he seemed lost. Humans were turned away from his house when the orisha insisted they had not made appointments with him. The ancient one was losing his memory, and with it, his ability to rule the world. Eshu was the first to run to Olófin to tell him, "The world is in trouble. Obatalá has lost his mind."

Olófin sat before Eshu, his arms crossed on his chest. "It is because he refused to make ebó, Eshu. What can I do?"

"If you don't do something the world will fall apart. Obatalá's ashé is what keeps it all glued together."

"I cannot force him to make ebó. He refused."

"Obatalá has lost his mind!" Eshu stood there defiantly. "He won't remember that he refused to make ebó. Just go to him and tell him it's time to make ebó. He might do it now."

Olófin thought about that. "It's not hard to fool a man who's lost his memory. We'll go. If it doesn't work, Obatalá won't be fit to rule anymore."

Together, Eshu and Olófin left for Obatalá's home on earth. On their way they grabbed handfuls of the leaves and seeds from the Iwereyeye.

They found Obatalá outside his home, wandering and half dressed. His eyes were vacant, his expression flat. He stood gazing at the plants and flowers that grew in his garden, looking at them much like a child seeing the world for the first time. Eshu's heart sank in his chest, and slowly, so as not to startle him, he walked to Obatalá's side while Olófin stood back and watched.

"Obatalá, how are you this morning?" Eshu extended his arms to embrace the old man, but he just stood there staring.

"Obatalá? You called me Obatalá. Is that my name?"

"It is," said Eshu.

"That's right. I am Obatalá. Why am I standing in the garden? I have a kingdom to run."

"You do," said Eshu, "but first you must make ebó so you have strength and wisdom to rule."

"Of course! Let us go make ebó." He stood unmoving. "What ebó?"

Olófin walked up to Obatalá holding branches of Iwereyeye. "We have to make ebó with this, old friend," he said.

Obatalá stared at the branches with its green leaves and red and black seeds. Obatalá took one of the branches from Olófin's hands; he held it to his nose and breathed deeply. It smelled of rain and damp earth. "This is funny," he said, looking at Eshu. "The seeds are dressed as you. Do you know this plant?"

"I was there when it was created," said Eshu. "It has great ashé. When Olófin is done you will have the strength to rule the world and everything in it."

Obatalá smiled a crooked smile; spittle dripped from the corner of his mouth. His eyes were wild. "Let us make ebó quickly! I have a world to rule!"

Eshu helped Olófin make ebó to Obatalá's head that day. They washed his head with omiero made from the leaves of Iwereyeye; and then they gave his orí cool, white things—coconut, cocoa butter, efun, and cotton. They pushed the seeds into the pulp on his head and wrapped it with white cloth. When they were done the fog lifted from Obatalá's eyes, and a single tear slid from the corner of one. "Oh no," he said. "What have I done?" He remembered the past weeks as if they were a dream, a nightmare from which he could not escape, and he fell to the earth at Olófin's feet. "I am so sorry! I almost ruined everything." Before Olófin could lift him he was crying, spasms rocking his body. Olófin blessed him, lifted him, and the two orishas, Eshu and Olófin, embraced him between them.

The sun went down in the garden that day with the two orishas comforting Obatalá. "Never again will I doubt your wisdom, Olófin."

The next day Obatalá had his gardeners plant the seeds of the Iwereyeye in his own garden; and it became the most favored of his plants. For Obatalá discovered that the plant did have ashé; even thought its seeds could not decide if they were red or black, such are things in the mind. They are always rolling and moving; thoughts are always one or the other, and with its ashé he never lost his memory again.

The Kingdom of Earth, the Kingdom of Heaven

From the Odu Obara Unle (6-8)

The great one does not eat out of the hands of the small one.

Shangó was riding his horse through the countryside when he saw Obatalá walking the same path. "Father, why do you walk?" he asked.

"Because I am too tired to run," said Obatalá. He smiled weakly.

Shangó jumped off his horse and helped Obatalá climb on. He took the reins and walked back toward Oyó. "It has been many years, father," he said. "So long that you have not seen my kingdom. Let me show you." Obatalá sat silently as he rode into town.

As Shangó entered Oyó the townspeople greeted him, parting so he could pass through with Obatalá and his white horse. In the center of town near his palace Shangó raised his arm to heaven and said, "My people! Show my father, Obatalá, that I am your king!" A great cry rose, thousands of voices cheering Shangó at once. It was deafening.

When the people went silent, Obatalá slid down from Shangó's horse. "Now, Shangó, let me show you my kingdom." Obatalá swept his arms to the sky and the heavens opened up. The spiritual world seemed to impose itself on the material; they were side by side, the seen and normally unseen. All the orishas and spirits in heaven bowed to Obatalá, and the people of Oyó bowed as well. Soon, even Shangó put his head to the earth.

Obatalá blessed them all.

As the rift between heaven and earth sealed, Shangó rose; his subjects remained prone. There was not a sound—even the wind stood still. "You are a greater king than I, Father. Even the spirits in heaven put their heads down to you."

"It is true—I am the king of heaven, Shangó. But as humble as you are, you will always be a king on earth."

Since that time, Shangó has been known as the King of the religion, and all oriatés in the religion become, while fulfilling their roles, Shangó's representatives on earth. For while Obatalá rules supreme in heaven, the head of all the orishas, Shangó by his decree rules supreme on earth, the head of all those who worship the orishas. Obatalá gave him that because of his humility before the kingdom of heaven.

7
PATAKÍS FROM THE COMPOSITES OF ODÍ

Iroko, the Tree of Life
From the Odu Odí Ogundá (7-3)

*He who wants blessings in old age
should pray wishfully and fervently for
himself while still young.*

"It is your turn to leave heaven and go into the world below," said the young diviner to Iroko. He sat on his haunches on a thin, grass mat while Iroko sat slightly above him on a wooden stool. "All the orishas have gone before you. Some have lived mortal lives and returned already. They bring with them incredible tales from the material world."

Iroko's eyes narrowed. The diviner shuddered under his gaze. Those eyes were black and vacant like the darkness of space. They betrayed no emotion; and like dark pools of water, they returned the young man's own shadowy reflection. He watched himself in the orisha's eyes.

"What have I to do with that world?" asked Iroko, his voice hollow. "I have always been here, in heaven. I was here when the earth was born. I know when it was made. I know how it was made. I even know when it will end. I know all its secrets."

Eshu sat at the young diviner's side whispering in his ear. The young man pursed his lips in worry. A diviner had to speak truth—that of the odu and that of Eshu—and there were times that speaking the truth felt dangerous. Times such as now, when he sat at the feet of a powerful orisha. "Eshu says you awakened when the world was born, as did all the orishas in heaven. You are Irunmole, one of the firstborn. But you were not there when Olódumare awakened. You did not see the mysteries to which only Eshu and Orúnmila were privy. And it is your place, as it is the place of all the orishas, to go down in the world below and experience what the material world has to offer."

"But why?" He spoke as if it was a question, yet the force behind his voice made it clear he was demanding an answer from both Eshu and the young diviner.

"We are all parts of Olódumare, my friend. As we experience and grow, so does he. It is the ashé of all spirits in heaven to be born at least once. And it is your turn." The diviner sat still, rolling ibó in his hands.

"I have every comfort right here, in heaven. If I leave, how do I know I will be as comfortable on the earth?"

Eshu broke his silence and spoke directly to Iroko, "Your odu promises prosperity on the earth. Odí Ogundá says you will be wealthy and well known among your peers. But that prosperity comes with sacrifice. Before you leave heaven you must make ebó to me. Offer me all types of animals and fruits. Be generous with your gifts, for as you sacrifice so shall you prosper. But know that once you descend into the world, your prosperity will be slow in coming. You will suffer greatly before you prosper. You must learn to have patience, and you must learn to honor me by saying, 'Maferefún Eshu,' every day that you live on the earth. Do this and one day you will be among the most loved and revered orishas in the world."

Iroko was silent. His face betrayed no emotion. "This is your destiny," said the young diviner.

"And who am I to fight destiny?" asked Iroko. As if it was his decision to make all along he said, "I will make sacrifice to Eshu. And I will venture out into the world. I will be patient, and I will honor Eshu each day that I live on the earth. I will seek out my fortune. Consider it done." He left the diviner and Eshu sitting alone at the mat while he left to find the items needed for his ebó.

Eshu laughed and whispered to the diviner, "Now Iroko will learn humility and patience. Once he has learned his lesson, only then will I give him the prosperity he craves."

By nightfall his ebó was complete and Iroko crossed the gate that separated earth and heaven.

Iroko found himself in darkness, covered by dirt. He was unable to move or speak. When rain fell from the sky he got wet and muddy; when the sun bore down on the earth he got hot. In time he felt himself swell in the darkness; he felt the earth around him give way as he grew. Reaching deep into himself for strength he reached for the surface and broke through the soil.

He was a sapling, a young tree newly born. Even though he had no mouth to speak, as he felt the cool air on his skin he thought, "Maferefún Eshu! Today I am born to the world." Then he looked around and saw that he was growing in the midst of a great garbage dump. Acrid, rotting smells filled the cool air, and he watched, unable to move or speak as humans brought baskets and pails of waste and threw them at his feeble roots. Some even relieved themselves among the rubbish before walking away into the forest. No one paid any mind to the young tree that grew slowly in the midst of the garbage.

But grow he did. Instead of being bitter at his fate, Iroko did what he promised to do each day that he lived. In his mind he paid homage to Eshu, the phrase "Maferefún Eshu" becoming both a prayer and a mantra as the years rolled by.

Quietly, where Iroko could neither see nor hear him, Eshu laughed. "He learns patience well!" he told himself.

Generations passed and with them Iroko languished in the ever-growing rubbish dump. As he grew, thousands of seeds ripened in his branches and the winds scattered these at his feet. Slowly, they burrowed into the earth and emerged as saplings, growing tall and strong around their father-tree. Iroko's roots intertwined with theirs and the loneliness he felt was abated. Every morning and every night he whispered, "Maferefún Eshu." Truly, he was thankful for the blessing of his own children on the earth. There, surrounded by the garbage and waste of humans the Iroko-forest grew.

One morning Eshu passed by the dump and saw the great trees growing, and he heard all the trees whispering in the wind, "Maferefún Eshu."

"After all these generations, has the ancient Iroko finally learned humility? And he has taught it to his own children?" Eshu smiled, for indeed he had.

This was at the time when humans were still building their homes from mud and straw; and when the weather grew severe their houses would tumble down with the wind and the rain. Eshu walked to the elder of the nearest village and saw he was crying over his own home. It had come down during a great rainstorm. "There is a way to build stronger houses," Eshu told the wise man.

"How?" he asked.

"In the dump grow great, strong trees whose wood withstands the passage of time. If you were to build your homes from logs and timbers taken from those trees your homes could withstand even the greatest storms."

The elder saw the wisdom of the plan. "Thank you, Eshu. But how can we get to the trees when they are surrounded by so much trash?"

"Have the youth of your town work to clear it all away."

Again, he saw the brilliance of that. He tried to put his head on the ground to the great orisha, but Eshu stopped him. "No need, you seem almost as old as I, old man." The two embraced, and Eshu held him at arm's length. "But there are two things upon which I must insist."

"Anything," said the old man.

"First, save the seeds from each tree you cut down and plant them throughout the world. It is the only way to make sure each generation has enough for its own use, and still enough to carry forward into the centuries that follow."

"Agreed," said the old man.

"Second, the oldest tree stands in the middle of the dump. Its trunk reaches up into the heavens. That is the eldest of all the Iroko that exist in the world, the father of them all. Save that tree as a shrine to the ancient spirit of the Iroko. Never cut it down, but leave offerings there for the gift of strong houses it brings you. Thus will you always be blessed."

It did not take long for the youth to clean away the garbage dump, and as Eshu said, they built their houses from its wood. Seeds were planted throughout the world and great forests grew from these. And the father of them all, the ancient Iroko who first set roots in the center of the dump, became revered as a great orisha. In time he was wealthy and had great coins and jewels and trinkets set among his roots.

For the Iroko had learned humility, and he became the greatest orisha on the earth. In time, Iroko became the symbol for serving Olódumare, Olorún, and Olófin, and the orishas themselves nestled at his roots.

How the Birds Got Their Wings
From the Odu Odí Obara (7-6)

The fastest way to safety is to fly away
from danger.

It was early morning, the time just after dawn when the birds hopped down from their trees to scavenge the earth for bugs and worms. This was the safest time for them, the time when predators slept in their dens, exhausted from a night of stalking sleeping prey; and because there was safety in numbers they blanketed the forest. The only sound was that of their small feet hopping over dry leaves, or the occasional snap of a twig under their feet. Each ate its fill, and then began the slow climb back up to the highest branches.

There came a growl from deeper in the forest, and then screams as a leopard sprang from the shadows. Hundreds of birds scrambled for the trees while others tried to hide in the underbrush. The leopard's attack was swift, and soon the forest was filled with feathers and blood as he ate his fill. For none of the birds had wings—they were tiny, helpless creatures who could climb, but none could fly. When the attack ended the leopard lay on the forest floor beneath the survivors; he sat there licking his paws and then his face. Snapping his tongue over his teeth, he got up and lumbered back into the forest.

The birds looked down where they had been feeding—the feathers of their brothers and sisters still floating on light breezes. When they were sure the leopard was gone, one little bird was the first to speak, "We need to see the diviners. We need to make ebó. We cannot live like this any longer. One day, we will be wiped off the face of the earth."

The other birds agreed.

It was late afternoon before they gathered their courage to travel. They hopped from branch to branch, a great, chirping cloud that moved through the canopy. When they came to the edge of the forest, one by one they dropped to the earth and ran toward the city. Not even the leopard had the courage to travel there. Humans had weapons and would kill the overgrown cat on sight. The birds were small, tiny, and humans regarded them with curious ease as they moved, in mass, to the old diviner's home.

Mofá was surprised to see hundreds of birds outside his front door. "What are you all doing here?" he asked.

The little bird that spoke first in the forest spoke first to the old man. "We have come to see you, Mofá. We want you to divine for us, and we want to make ebó. The leopard hunts us relentlessly, and if it continues the day will come when we are no more on the earth."

He opened his door wide and invited the creatures inside. They blanketed his sitting room while he took the smallest bird back to his divination room. After a lengthy prayer to the orishas, he cast his cowries on the mat and marked the letter that fell. "Odí Obara, 7-6 in the diloggún. Indeed, you must make ebó if you are to survive!"

"What must we do?" asked the little bird.

"Bring me a rat, a fish, a young chicken, and a rooster. Bring me sticks and twigs and dried leaves from the ground. We will make ebó to Elegguá, and he will save you and all your kind from death."

The birds canvassed the village looking for the items for their ebó. None of the humans touched them; they regarded them with a careful curiosity as they saw them all entering and leaving Mofá's home. They knew something special was in the works. Early that evening as the sun slid down the western sky, Mofá finished their ebó and gave to each bird a packet of powder. "Go home," he said. "And before you go to sleep rub this powder over your bodies. Stay home for seven days—do not go anywhere on the ground, but stay high in the trees. When you wake up the morning of the eighth day there will be the miracle you seek."

The birds thanked the diviner and ran back to the forest; they climbed the tree closest to its edge and ran over the twigs and branches and leaves. Every morning when they awoke, they ate only the nuts and berries and bugs they could catch high in the trees; and every morning, the leopard, looking hungrier and hungrier, ran through the woods looking for the birds. So it went for seven days.

On the morning of the eighth day, the birds awoke to find wings had sprouted over their bodies, and as they tried to climb down the trees their wings began to flap—they took flight.

Since that day the leopard has given up trying to feed on the birds, because when he sees one sitting on the earth, before he gets to it the bird has flapped its wings and taken flight.

And that is how the birds got their wings. They made ebó and took to the skies.

How The Maraca Was Born
From the Odu Odí Obara (7-6)

*The peony seed cannot decide if it is red
or if it is black.*

Olófin created the rosary bead plant; Eshu blessed it, and Obatalá decreed it was one of the greatest plants in the religion. Soon it was decreed by the orishas that any plant missing in their sacred omiero could be replaced with its leaves, and all the orishas planted it in their gardens. Shangó had one such bush growing outside his bedroom window. Obatalá gave him the seeds and he planted them carefully where they would receive ample amounts of sunshine and rain. It grew quickly, and thousands of seeds grew in its branches.

The day came that one of the seeds looked at all the seeds to his left and saw only red, and then he turned his eyes to the right and saw only black. "We are the strangest bush in all the land," said the seed, "for all of you on my left are red and all of you on my right are black." He tried to see his own color, but no matter how he tried to twist or turn he could not see himself. "What color am I?" he wondered aloud. "Am I red or am I black?"

One of the seeds to his left answered him first, "You are black. I can see you from where I sit and you are most definitely black, just like all the seeds to your right."

"Thank you, red seed," said the peony, and he shifted himself to lay closer to his black brethren on his right.

"You are not one of us!" said the seed to his right. "For I can see your color clearly from where I hang, and you are most definitely red. You belong on the other side with all the red seeds."

"He is black!" roared the other seed. "He belongs with you!"

"You don't belong with us either," screamed another seed further right. "For I see you clearly, and you are red as is the first seed. Move over to your side!"

Soon all the seeds were fighting about who was red and who was black. None of them thought, not for a minute, that maybe they were half each color. Outside Shangó's bedroom window the seeds argued through the night. Shangó could neither rest nor sleep and when he could stand the argument no longer he ran outside with a large gourd and yelled, "Enough! You are all the same color—half red and half black!" He grabbed the seeds by the handful and put them inside the gourd; he bound it tight. "Now you are neither red nor black; you live in darkness and without light there can be no color. Be quiet!"

The seeds, however, continued to quarrel, but inside the gourd their cacophony became harmony. Shangó shook the gourd and listened to the sound the seeds made; it pleased him. In that moment, the maraca was born. Shangó stashed the maraca inside his house far away from his bedroom and slept peacefully all that night. The next day, he shared the instrument with all the orishas, and soon most of them preferred the sound of the maraca above all others.

Still, the peony seeds never decided if they were red or if they were black, and they remained the same throughout all their days.

The Pact of the Hand and the Anus

From the Odu Odí Meji (7-7)

*To find good fortune everyone and
everything must work together.*

There was a time when humans defecated like animals; they would squat and be done. Yet the bugs and flies—these were attracted to the scent left behind —and the humans were miserable.

One day the anus spoke to its human, "I am miserable. I spend all my days working to cleanse your body of waste, but the bugs and flies—they follow me. My odor is bad and I cannot cleanse myself. Let us make a pact."

"And what would that pact be?" asked the human. He, too, was overwhelmed by the insects attracted to the odor of his anus.

"I will continue to do what I do; I will cleanse your body of waste. And once I am done, you will have your right hand cleanse me so that the flies and bugs will leave us alone."

It took no time for the human to consent, and the next time he defecated he took one of the leaves of the forest and wiped his anus clean. When the flying insects left him alone, all the humans in the world learned from what he did, and they did the same.

For this, they used their right hands.

In time, the first human who learned to clean his anus came to the shrine of Shangó to make ebó; and with his right hand, he reached up to Shangó's implements to leave his favorite adimú—amalá. Shangó was appalled.

"Stop!" he ordered. The human stood there holding the gourd of cooked cornmeal in his right hand. "I have seen what you do with that hand," said Shangó. "You defecate, and then with your right hand you wash your anus. I cannot take any food offered by the right hand. Make me another dish of amalá, and offer it to me with your left."

The human did as he was told. He washed his hands, and cooked amalá for Shangó. When he approached his shrine, the orisha's ebó was held in the left hand and not the right. Since that day not only have humans washed their anus after defecating, but also they have washed their hands; and when offering any ebó to Shangó, they bring it to him in their left.

Simply, it is the way things should be.

8
PATAKÍS FROM THE COMPOSITES OF UNLE

The Rock and the Cactus

From the Odu Unle Okana (8-1)

The cactus grows where nothing
else will.

There was a time when the rock and the cactus were friends; they lived side by side in the desert. But the day came when the rock and the cactus wanted the same piece of land, and they began to argue.

"You can live anywhere," argued the cactus. "You are a rock, and all you need to do is sit still and just be. I have to have sunlight. I have to have water. I have to have earth in which to spread my roots. You have no such needs."

"I was here first," said the rock. "I don't move; I don't grow. I don't create seeds that scatter on the winds. I have sat here since the beginning of time, and I will be here, in this same spot, at the end of time. You must go live somewhere else."

Sadly, the cactus looked over the desert and saw that all the best places for him to grow were covered by rocks. Not knowing what else to do he sought out the diviner Mofá. "If you make ebó," promised the wise diviner, "you will conquer the rock and be able to live anywhere and everywhere you want in the desert. The rock will not be able to stop you."

So the cactus did as he was told and made ebó. His ashé changed that same day. He found that he could set down roots everywhere in the desert, even in places covered by rocks, and he would grow and prosper while the rock stood silently beneath him, living in his shadow.

That is why, today, one can find the cactus growing anywhere and everywhere in the desert, even in places overrun by rocks.

How the Moon Fooled the Sun and Saved the Earth
From the Odu Unle Ejioko (8-2)

A star occupies only the place that God commanded.

There are certain truths about our world that we take for granted: Every day the sun rises, dispensing light and warmth over the earth, and by night the moon glows, surrounded softly by thousands of sparkling stars all nestled in space. The day warms us: the night cools us. There is balance.

Things were not always like this.

Before there was light there was only darkness, and Olódumare knew that for life to flourish there must be light. He reached into space with his mighty hands and fashioned the sun to shine by day and the moon to shine by night. Adding to the beauty of the night sky, he created thousands of stars, shiny pinpoints of light suspended in the heavens. But the sun seemed lonely, and the daytime sky seemed barren, so Odúduwa went behind Olódumare, creating stars to accompany the sun.

Odúduwa was pleased. Olódumare watched.

At first, the days were warm, and the nights were cold. As time passed, the days grew hot and the nights cool. As centuries flew by, the sun gained strength, and his children—his stars—grew in size and strength as well. The moon's children, the nighttime stars, were delicate; and they remained so. Slowly the daytime sky grew brighter and brighter; the days grew hotter and hotter, and the nights were unable to cool the excessive heat suffusing the earth.

The world suffered.

The heat kept the rains away and fresh water grew scarce. Plants were the first to wither and die; and the animals that fed on those suffered from hunger. Animals who ate other animals soon found their prey in short supply, and the humans who depended on both for sustenance panicked. With scant food, people knew fear, hunger, and thirst. A great cry rose to heaven, wails of suffrage that rocked its gates.

Olófin heard their cries. Worried, he descended to earth, followed by the orishas.

Together they walked through the oppressive heat. The sky blazed with a thousand fires burning so fiercely that it hurt their eyes to look toward heaven. Beside a river that was all but dry lay a young woman, and when she saw Olófin and all the orishas walking the earth she pleaded through parched lips, "We are dying. Help us."

Olófin was silent while he thought; the orishas were silent, waiting for Olófin to speak. Finally he said, "Gather those who remain, and make ebó here at the river. Gather thousands of white stones, and paint them white again so they glow the most brilliant white you have ever seen. After all the stones are painted and dry, leave them here on the riverbank, and sacrifice a white hen and a white rooster. I will save you."

Because the day was too hot to work, the humans waited until night to make their ebó. The moon looked down from heaven and saw their suffering; and she saw the humans come together at the river to make ebó. Her heart broke because she was no longer able to cool the stifling heat, so she removed herself from the skies and went to Olófin's palace where she pleaded with him to save the world.

The humans had just finished their ebó when the moon disappeared from the night sky. It was the first lunar eclipse, and they were in awe. "Olófin's power is great," muttered the young woman who had begged him for his help. "Surely, we will be saved."

The moon arrived at Olófin's palace, and the wise old man smiled as she greeted him by prostrating herself on the floor. Strong hands touched her lightly on her shoulders, and even stronger arms lifted her. They embraced. "Olófin," she whispered in his ear, almost afraid to speak, "Everyone suffers on earth. My nights are no longer cool, and great waves of heat build stronger each day. Everything is dying, and I am afraid it is my fault."

Olófin broke the embrace gently, holding the moon at arm's length. "It is not your fault." His voice was gentle and reassuring. "The stars in the daytime sky have grown strong like their father. The world can't sustain such heat. But there is something you can do to help."

"Anything!" A single tear slid down her face.

"Go to the river and sacrifice a rooster and a hen, both white. Take the biggest gourd you can find. After you make ebó you will know what to do."

For the remainder of the night, the moon was on the earth, making ebó where she watched the humans make their own ebós. She saw all the beautiful white stones they left on the riverbank; and she noticed that in her subtle glow, they sparkled like her own small children, the stars who lived in the nighttime sky. As she pondered this, Odúduwa came to her.

"Moon, do you know the stars in the daytime sky are destroying the world?" It was more of a statement than a question.

"Yes, I know."

"Many years ago," he said, "Olódumare created all things. He put the sun in the daytime sky, and the moon and stars in the nighttime sky. I thought things were unbalanced, so I myself created the stars in the day. I thought myself as wise as Olódumare." Odúduwa's voice trailed off, and for a moment he was silent. "I was foolish. I should have left well enough alone. The world was beautiful as it was."

The Moon cried as she listed to Odúduwa's story. A single tear struck a white stone, and its glow intensified. She studied it. "I came here to make ebó for the world. Olófin told me to sacrifice a white rooster and a white hen to the river, and he told me I would know what to do. But I've made my ebó, and I still don't know how I can help."

"Olófin wanted you to come see what the humans did for yourself." He waved his arms over the thousands of white stones, and then pointed at the gourd the moon brought with her. "There is already a plan. Put all these stones in the gourd you carry. Take them back to heaven."

"I cannot carry all these stones in this gourd. There are thousands of them. My gourd could hold maybe a dozen."

"Trust me, your gourd will hold all the stones," Odúduwa said with a knowing gleam in his eyes.

The moon gathered the stones one by one and tossed them into the gourd. Mysteriously, it held them all.

She eyed it wearily. "It held all the stones," she gasped. "But surely it is too heavy for me to carry back into the sky."

"Trust me," said Odúduwa. "It is light enough for you to carry."

She picked it up; it weighed no more than an empty gourd.

"Now listen carefully, because mortal creatures cannot live another day though this heat. When the sun begins to rise, call out to him. Tell him that the earth is dying because of your children and his. Then you will make a proposal with the sun to save the earth.

You will suggest to him that each of you will throw your children into the river, and you will match child-for-child as they fall from the skies. Only you will not destroy your own children, for they give beauty to the night sky and do not destroy life on the earth. Instead, you will throw a single white stone, and the sun will think that it is your child. Tell him to throw his children into the river as you do the same."

The Moon took the stone-filled gourd and returned to the sky. As the Sun rose that morning, she did as she was told. She cried out across the heavens, "Sun, our children are too hot; they burn too brightly in the skies and are destroying all life on the earth. But we can save it, and the world will love us for it! We can sacrifice our own children; the world will cool, and every living thing will hallow our names!"

The Sun knew it was true; his children were destroying the earth. But he was happy that the Moon thought her children were causing trouble as well. "You are a wise woman, Moon," the Sun called out. "Let us do as you suggest; let us sacrifice our children to the river and save the world!" One by one, the Sun threw his children into the river; there, the water destroyed the star. And the Moon matched his one to one, only instead of a child, a star, she threw a stone, and it burned in the earth's atmosphere as it fell into the river and was destroyed.

This marked the birth of the falling stars, balls of fire that fall from the sky and burn up before striking the earth.

It took hours, but before the day was over the Sun had sent all his children to their death while the Moon had sent only stones.

That night as the moon rose, one by one her stars began to shine. The sun realized he had been deceived, and he was angry; but since he was of the day, and she of the night, there was nothing he could do. For the first time in years, the night was cool, not hot. The humidity in the air coalesced; the rains fell. Rivers filled. Crops grew. Thirst and hunger were sated, and life rejoiced.

And Odúduwa never again tried to second-guess Olódumare's wisdom.

The Waxing and Waning of the Moon
From the Odu Unle Ogundá (8-3)

*When we war with our own head, one of
us is always the loser.*

When it was time for the moon to leave heaven and live in the night-time sky, she consulted with Elegguá. The moon hoped for a long, prosperous life, and she wanted to know what she had to do to maintain her blessings.

"One as fair as you need not worry about her fate anywhere," Elegguá said.

"Thank you, Elegguá. You are too kind. But I want to be prosperous in the material world."

Elegguá divined for the moon. "Your growth and prosperity in the world is assured," he said. "For you will be born to light man's way through darkness, and every day that you live you will grow greater. You will inspire lovers; you will console the weary; and, there are those who will worship you." He stopped, and frowned, looking down at the cowries on his mat. "But your light will not last forever. It will wane unless you make ebó."

"What is the ebó I must make?" she asked, almost fearful.

"I want a goat, a jutía, and a rooster. I want smoked fish, and all kinds of fresh fruits. I want honey and rum and cigars. Give me all these things, and I will make sure that your light will never wane, and you will live forever among the stars!"

Graciously, she smiled at Elegguá. "I will make ebó," she said.

Although the moon was a beautiful bright spirit, inside she was cold and greedy. A part of her wanted to make ebó; a part of her told her making ebó was futile. The moon warred with her own head over this. Before leaving heaven she gave the rum, honey, and cigars to Elegguá, but she did not sacrifice the goat, rooster, or jutía. "That is enough for him," she reasoned. "Elegguá wants too much."

At first, in the night sky she was no more than a sliver, a slice of light no brighter than the faintest star; but night after night, her strength grew and with it her light. It took two weeks' time, but soon she hung proudly in the night sky, casting a silvery light to dispel the darkness. The moon was quite beautiful, and she was happy.

Lovers loved. Poets dreamed. Some worshipped her. It was all Elegguá said it would be.

Even Elegguá enjoyed roaming the earth under the light of the full moon. One night he was licking his honey, drinking his rum, and smoking his cigars when his stomach rumbled. "I'm hungry," he said. "Where is my food?"

Elegguá looked everywhere, but he could not find his goat or his rooster or his jutía. "The moon did not leave me anything to eat?" He was in disbelief. When his hunger deepened, he was angry.

Elegguá hid in the shadow of a tree and watched the moon for quite some time. As she began her nightly descent he thought, "She is a greedy spirit, wanting to be perfect in the material realm without making ebó. Two weeks is enough—it is time for her beauty to fade." Sucking in a long, slow breath, Elegguá pursed his lips at the moon and blew with all his might. As the moon slid below the horizon, she lost just a bit of her glow.

For the next two weeks, every night the moon shrank in size until she was so small no one could see her. It was then that she finished her sacrifices of a goat, a rooster, a jutía, and smoked fish. Out of fear, she gave Elegguá everything he requested as ebó. But, it was too late to lock in all her blessings; and although she waxed again, she always waned.

That is why for two weeks every lunar month, the moon grows until she is full and beautiful, and then for two weeks every lunar month, she shrinks until there is nothing left. She refused to make all of her ebó when Elegguá asked; and as she was told in heaven, her beauty forever waxed and waned.

Ekún* Fails to Make Ebó
From the Odu Unle Ogundá (8-3)

*The biggest blessing is to know one's place
in the world, and accept it.*

Heaven was a place of peace and prosperity. No one wanted; no one thirsted; no one hungered. Lured by the promises of the blue jewel hanging in space, one by one everyone and everything in heaven made their descent to the new world. Oceans filled first with exotic aquatics; the land grew green and lush with the grasses and vines and trees; and the forest filled with wild animals whose forms were as varied as the stars were innumerable.

As everything took form and substance, something curious happened in the world when animals took the flesh.

Those who were small and weak in heaven became great and powerful on the earth. Those who made ebó became predators, while those who forgot to offer ebó became prey. Friends were divided by hunger, tooth, and claw, and a great cry went through the universe.

It was time for Ekún to cross; he was an intelligent spirit, and not wanting to be prey he went to Unle to make ebó. The wise diviner opened the odu that morning, and as the letters rolled onto the mat he was pleased. "You are blessed, Ekún," he said with a smile. "The world of flesh will bring you strength. Wealth waits for you. A huge family waits for you. Power will be yours."

Ekún, who was the leopard, smiled.

"Still, nothing in the material world comes without cost."

"I will pay what I must to have what is mine!" Hungrily, he bit his lip slightly, and then ran his tongue over the single drop of blood his teeth drew. It was all reflex; there was no thought behind any of it,

---

*Ekún is the Lucumí/Yoruba word for leopard.

and when Ekún realized what he was doing he froze. "I feel something inside," he told Unle. "It's a slight rumbling, almost a need. I've never felt it before."

"Your flesh on earth takes form even now, while you sit at the mat. You will not be in heaven much longer," said Unle. "Quickly, before you go to earth you must sacrifice to Ogún. Offer him a goat, two roosters, two pigeons, and a guinea hen. At the crossroad that separates heaven from earth, you must sacrifice to Elegguá. Offer him a goat, a rooster, and a guinea hen. Once you are on earth, you must again offer a sacrifice to Ogún. Offer him a monkey. This will ensure your wealth and stability."

Ekún's jaw dropped, and he let out a loud sound that was almost a roar. It surprised him, and he slapped a hand across his lips. He never made that sound before, and suddenly he was afraid. "I must sacrifice a monkey? I must kill my friend, Obo?"* His voice was cold and angry. "Here in heaven, Obo and I have always been the best of friends. He was always good to me. I intend to remain friends with him on earth; surely our bond cannot be broken by impending descent? How can I sacrifice my own best friend?"

The odu took a deep breath and explained, "Things on the earth are a reflection of heaven, it's true, but when spiritual beings take on the flesh in the mortal world, their natures change." He looked into the leopard's eyes, waiting for acknowledgment. There was none. But Unle could feel Ekún's new nature taking hold; even at the mat he was slowly assimilating the form and features he would have on the earth.

"Here, we all live, and we live freely, and we all live harmoniously. There is no sickness. There is no old age. There is no death. Energy and ashé are exchanged liberally. It will not be like this on earth. Life will feed on life. To keep balance everything will be food for something else, and there will be sickness, disease, and death. And your nature will change. It has already changed while you sat here at the mat seeking

---

*Obo is a Lucumí/Yoruba word for monkey.

your destiny. It is your destiny to be a powerful hunter, the predator of all things in the animal kingdom. You are meant to be at the top of the food chain, and you yourself will feed on all things—including Obo. Few will feed on you. It is how Olódumare created the world. It is the nature Olódumare imbued in you. You will see."

With narrowed eyes and a cold heart, Ekún thanked the diviner, but his gratitude was not sincere, and as he waited for Olódumare to send him to earth he contemplated all he was told. Ekún decided, "Everyone who makes ebó prospers, but those who do not, they fail. I will make ebó. I will do all that Unle asked. But I will not sacrifice my friend. This cannot be the will of God, for friend should not kill friend."

By the time he finished his ebó he was on earth. As the diviner promised, his form was changed.

He was long and lean, muscled elegantly; his legs were solid and tight, his trunk hard and thick. Across his body was a spotted pelt whose colors melted into the forest's undergrowth when he hid. In spite of his strength he was agile, able to slink silently through the forest. His claws were long and sharp like small daggers, and his teeth were razor edged, perfect for shredding flesh. Sharp eyes and a keen nose made him the most powerful hunter.

He knew what hunger was, and he knew instinctively that only warm, raw meat would sate its rumbling. It was on the hunt that he met his wife; quickly her belly ripened with children, and Ekún knew it was time to find a home and settle down.

"I will make my ebó to Ogún now," he thought. His new predatory instincts took hold, and the leopard was willing to do anything for the good of himself and his family.

What Ekún did not know was this: Obo's nature on earth changed as well. He went to the diviners to make ebó before leaving heaven, and Unle divined for him as he had Ekún. Obo was afraid of the fate that was his, to be weak and preyed upon on the earth, so he not only made ebó, he also doubled ebó, and gave Elegguá everything he asked for, and everything he could want. Plied by his offerings, Elegguá changed his fate in life, making him agile, strong, and sly. While he was prey, now he was intelligent prey, and only with great cunning would any animal feast on his flesh. On earth, he realized few predators could climb trees, and Obo spent all his days and all his nights swinging and sleeping in branches, lazily eating the fruits that ripened out of the reach of predators.

While Ekún was a fierce hunter he could not climb, and by the time he decided to make his ebó, Obo had skills that no other animal could match. No matter how much he tracked the monkey, the leopard never caught him. His ebó remained undone. He lived his life on earth, wanderer in the forest, living as a brutal beast and not a creature of elegance and prosperity.But that is what happens when one neither makes nor completes ebó. Blessings promised are blessings lost.

The Tale of Cotton

From the Odu Unle Irosun (8-4)

If we would listen to the teachings of odu,
we would last like our ancestors lasted; if
we would follow the teachings that odu
has to offer us, we would grow old like
the ancient ones did.

It was late when the witches took form; they flew through the night as graceful birds, in numbers so large and with feathers so dark, they blotted out the stars. One by one they gathered in the branches of the Iroko tree, outnumbering even its leaves. For tonight was a special night; it was their monthly gathering, and they had business to discuss—the destruction of the plant known as *cotton*.

Of all the spirits that took form on earth, it was the cotton plant that annoyed them the most. With its green foliage and delicate purple flowers it had a beauty by day that was haunting. At night, its sweet scent was intoxicating, almost delicious, a gentle perfume that pervaded the night with hints of both the exotic and mundane. Humans regarded that simple plant as one of the world's most useful, for from its seedpods burst soft gauzy wads that they wove into the most beautiful fabrics. Cotton himself was lost in his own arrogance; he flaunted his beauty and his usefulness even to the witches who flew through the night air.

So there, in the boughs of the Iroko, the witches decided to kill him and all his children, wiping them all off the face of the earth. Yet Cotton was blessed by all the orishas, and because of the blessings bestowed on him from heaven itself, he was powerful in his own way. It would take more than their magic to destroy such a creature.

First, the witches flew to their mother in the night sky, the moon, and begged her to help them with their evil. The moon agreed to help her children, and promised to send a storm wherever the cotton grew; the rains would fall, and they would not stop until the plant rotted beneath the flood. Yet the witches knew they needed more than just the power of the moon to destroy Cotton, so the next day they braved the heat and went before the sun. He himself owed many favors to the witches, so he promised that by day, when the moon had no power over the earth, he would send down his rays to boil and scorch the waters under which the cotton plant lay, and he would not stop until all the plant's leaves were withered. With the strongest allies of both the day and the night working with them, the witches knew Cotton's existence would be plagued, but plagued and cursed was not enough. They wanted extinction, so they continued to seek allies.

The birds called upon the worms that burrowed through the earth, and all the creeping, crawling things that would not emerge in either the light of day or the darkness of night. All these feared the witches, and they agreed to help: both day and night, they would gnaw at the roots of the cotton plant, and suck the juices from his stems while he lay helpless in the earth. To the wind did the witches call, and the winds, who were slaves to their chants and charms, agreed to blow and blow wherever Cotton grew until it was ripped from the earth's breast. Then the witches' pacts were done: fire, water, air, and earth all agreed to lend them their power, and they began their work. At night, late, one by one the birds descended on the earth wherever Cotton grew, and they began to feast on his seeds. With no viable seeds hiding in the earth, Cotton would not reproduce. The onslaught began, and the witches, as birds, sang gleefully. It was a joyous song tinged with insanity.

The witches forgot that plants were spirit as well, powerful beings that descended from heaven to live on the earth. As nature rose against him, Cotton trembled, and his spirit ripped free from the plants and fled to the house of the great diviner, Mofá. Trembling against the cold winds and icy rains, he beat on the old man's door, and Mofá let him in. Gently, he wrapped Cotton in white cloth woven from his own fibers, and offered him a seat.

"It is a horrible night out there for beast and spirit alike," said the wise man. "And I am sure the plants fare no better."

Cotton trembled. "It is only I who suffers. The witches have cursed me. They seek to destroy me."

"I know," he said, sitting on his mat and inviting Cotton to do the same. "The witches hate you for your arrogance. They hate you for your beauty." For what seemed hours Mofá simply watched Cotton's face, and Cotton trembled. As his plants suffered, so did he, and no amount of warm drink or blankets would free him from that chill. Finally, "You are too important to allow the witches to destroy you. Ebó can solve almost anything."

Mofá threw his cowries on the mat several times in succession, sometimes frowning, sometimes smiling, and when he was done he told the spirit, "We must rogate your head to cure you of your arrogance, and you must make ebó when we are done. From your own fibers, weave your own thread; and from your own thread, weave white cloth. From your own white cloth, and with your white threads, sew a new white robe for Obatalá. Leave this at the foot of the highest hill you can find, on a rock, and return to your plants. Let Obatalá do the rest."

Cotton spent the night at Mofá's house creating thread and weaving cloth and sewing robes; his arms shook and his fingers trembled as the dark storm outside sapped the strength from his physical form, the plants, but when morning came he was done. The rains ended; but now a white-hot sun bore down on the earth, and Cotton panted and grew weak from its heat. Mofá blessed him. "Go quickly to the hill and leave the robes. Return to your plants. Obatalá will seek you out. Have faith."

Faith was all Cotton had left as his strength waned.

Obatalá was traveling the road from heaven to earth that morning, and as his feet touched the ground his robes were splashed with mud. Carefully the old man walked, but each step splashed water and stained his white cloth. By the time he stood at the foot of the hill he was filthy. It was then he saw the bundle of robes sitting on a rock, with his name written clearly on a piece of paper. Obatalá smiled. "Who did this?" he asked no one.

The ground was dry and starting to parch as Obatalá traveled to town. He asked everyone he met who had left the robes for him on the rock by the hill, but everyone in town was afraid of the witches and no one dared whisper Cotton's name. Finally, Obatalá saw Mofá and he called out to the wise priest, "Mofá! Was it you who had foresight to leave me clean robes at the foot of the hill?"

"No, father," said Mofá. "It was a client, the plant named Cotton. The witches seek to destroy him, but he came to me and made ebó. Father —he is too important to the world to allow the witches to destroy him. From his plant came the very fabric you wear, and the clothes all of us in town wear. Without the cotton plant, we will be wearing animal skins again."

Obatalá went to a farm where thousands of the cotton plants lay wilted in the sun, and he called out to the plant's spirit, "Cotton, are you the one who wove and left new white clothing by the hillside?"

Weakly, Cotton's form materialized in front of the orisha. He was thin and his figure wavered in the hot sun. "Yes. It was I." The worms were eating at his roots, weakening him close to death. His voice was little more than a whisper. "The witches seek to destroy me. They have turned the sun, the moon, the wind, and the worms against me. I fear my time has come. It is too late and I will simply die."

Obatalá lifted his arms to the heavens and in a voice more powerful than the beating of the batá drums he said, *"Fun mi ashé lenu lati nsoro. Ashé tó, ashé bó, ashé bima! Ashé ishe'mi!"** The sky was clear, but thunder seemed to rumble in answer to the old man's voice. "From this day forth, all those who try to do you evil will be blinded by your purity, your whiteness, for now the cotton plant belongs to me, and not even the witches can claim ownership of or harm that which is mine!"

To this day the cotton plant is prolific and no one can destroy him.

The Calabash of Ashé
From the Odu Unle Odí (8-7)

Wisdom was scattered; ashé was spread;
and no one head holds it all.

Unle was on earth when he heard the call from the sky; it seemed to thunder over the earth, but in truth it only sounded inside his own head. "Return to us," it commanded. For a moment, he hesitated. *"Return? How am I to return? The only way back home . . . is to die . . ."* he thought. Before Unle could answer himself, he was home, in heaven, standing before Olódumare. The sudden change in the world around him left him dizzy, almost weak.

"Do not worry," said Olódumare. "The feeling will pass. I brought you here." Unle prostrated on the floor of God's great palace, a spacious

---

*"Give my tongue the ashé with which to speak. Ashé is sufficient; ashé envelops all; ashé is born. Ashé, work for me!"

room with walls awash in white light. Aged but strong, black hands tapped him on his shoulders, bidding him to rise. They embraced: Unle shuddered. God's ashé touched his skin lightly, but coursed through his body like a great thunderclap. When the embrace broke, it left him shaking.

From the corner of his eye, he saw a great calabash sitting on a stone pillar. Standing over it with hands raised was a strong, black man; from him issued streams of light, flowing into the porcelain container. "That is me, Unle."

The furrowed brow and puzzled expression betrayed Unle's sudden confusion. "Rather, that is me as Olorún, filling a great calabash with all the ashé the earth needs to survive." A lid appeared above the container, hovering, and the flowing lights were sucked into it as the lid slammed down on the calabash, sealing tight. The sound echoed, and for a moment, it felt as if all the air in the room was sucked into the sealed bowl as well.

The man was gone.

Olódumare walked to the stone pillar, his movement graceful and effortless. One moment, he was before Unle, and the next, he was simply standing beside the calabash. As if lifting a blade of grass, he carried the calabash to Unle.

"This cannot travel as easily as I summoned you, Unle," said Olódumare. "You must carry this back to the world with your own two hands; and, you must store it in a secret place until I tell you what to do with it. It is ashé, pure ashé, and the world will need it, if it is to survive what is to come."

Olódumare stretched out his hands, bidding Unle to take the calabash into his own. Unle put his hands on the container; it was warm and alive beneath his fingers. It sent shivers down his spine. Making sure Unle had a firm grasp, God removed his own hands, and suddenly the calabash became heavy, a burden for Unle to bear.

"I cannot hold it," he protested, and he bent at the knees, carefully lowering it to the floor.

"Stop. Do not set it down. You must carry it. Ashé is a heavy burden, but you must bear it and not set it down. And you must hide it safely on earth for me."

Unle left Olódumare's palace that day with a burden no man was strong enough to bear alone: all the ashé in the world. Each step from heaven to earth found that burden more cumbersome to carry. When, finally, Unle stepped foot on earth, the weight was unbearable, and the calabash fell from his hands.

As it fell, time seemed to slow, and horror crept over Unle's face. It hit the bare earth, and cracked; it shattered and the light that was within fled into the world. A great cry escaped Unle's lips; dread descended like night on his soul.

All the ashé was gone.

That day, everything on earth acquired ashé—wisdom, knowledge, and spiritual power—but because Unle let the calabash break, its acquisition was uneven and random. Even now, because no one man knows how much ashé was set free into the world, or how much ashé anything possesses, there is nothing in this world that should ever be underestimated, or considered inconsequential.

For that day, ashé was scattered, and no one person can hold it all. But if ashé is to ever consolidate again and save this world, all must learn how to share.

9

PATAKÍS FROM THE COMPOSITES OF OSÁ

How the Frog Got Its Poison

From the Odu Osá Ogundá (9-3)

He who makes ebó wins the war.

It was a hot summer night and the forest was sticky and humid. Any other night the snakes would have been sleeping, snuggled deep inside their bushes and burrows; but tonight the frogs were loud, and none of them could rest. Groggily they slithered across the damp forest floor, quietly so none could hear. Hundreds of them went to the riverbank, a great mass of coils so black that the frogs could not see them in the darkness. With no warning, not even a sound to betray them, the snakes lashed out at the frogs; death was painful, but quick.

The night was quiet again.

When morning came only one frog was left alive; from his hiding place in the reeds he watched as the snakes attacked his friends. Some were crushed in scaly coils before the snakes sucked them down while others were caught from behind, swallowed bit by bit while their eyes bulged in pain and fear. He trembled making no sounds; and as the morning sun slid up in the sky the snakes slithered away, their bellies full and bulging. Through the forest the frog hopped—away from the river, away from the place where the serpents massacred his friends. He hopped so hard and so long that he crashed into an old man who was out for a morning walk.

It was the diviner, Mofá.

Gently he lifted the frog in the palm of his hand. His skin was dry, his eyes distant. The little frog had hopped himself to exhaustion. "Watch where you run little friend," he said. "I could have crushed you under my feet."

The frog lay still in his hands.

"Why are you hopping so crazily?" he asked.

Slowly the frog's eyes focused on Mofá. His voice was soft when he spoke, "The snakes attacked us last night. They ate everyone. Except me."

"Since when do snakes eat frogs?" asked Mofá.

"Since they decided we were making too much noise."

Mofá sighed deeply. Frogs were gentle creatures with no way to protect themselves: they had long tongues for swallowing flies, but no teeth; they had strong legs for hopping, but no speed; they had small claws for climbing trees, but useless for fighting. Their skin was soft offering no protection from predators. If the snakes continued to eat them they would be wiped off the earth in no time.

"There is a way to protect yourselves," said Mofá. Still holding the frog, he walked off the path until they came to a thick bush laden with shiny black berries. He put the frog on the ground in front of the bush. "Eat these berries and the leaves," said Mofá, "and in time the snakes will bother your kind no more."

The frog recognized the bush; since he had been a young tadpole the other frogs told him never to touch it. "But those are poison! Any one of those berries or leaves will kill me."

"Have a bit of faith in me," the old man said. "Eat the berries and leaves from this bush. And no matter what happens, be humble. Neither boast nor brag about what you've done. You'll overcome the snakes. They will leave you and your kind alone forever."

Mofá left the frog alone with the bush. For quite some time he just eyed it.

As the sun set and darkness fell, the frog heard the snakes slithering in the forest. He trembled; and by accident he croaked. He went silent again, unmoving. "Just have faith," he told himself as he bit into the berries. The taste was bitter, almost metallic, and his throat constricted as the foul fluid went down. He waited a few moments to see if sickness would come, and when he realized he felt fine he ate more. With his toothless mouth he chewed on the leaves. It was the same—bitterness, constriction, and then nothing. "Perhaps these berries are not poison after all?" he asked himself. And then he felt a rumbling in his belly like gas; the pressure grew until he let out a loud, echoing croak.

The snake was close, closer than the frog knew, and when he heard the frog he attacked. One swift strike: there was pain, there were fangs, and for the frog, there was only darkness.

Something happened inside the snake's belly, something unfamiliar and fatal. At first there was the sour, metallic taste that the frog himself felt when he ate the berries; and then, his own throat constricted, much as the frog's throat had. Then there was pain, hot and cramping, and the snake vomited the frog so violently that he flew into the bush with a crash and a thud. As the little frog lay on the forest floor, dazed and confused, the snake coiled in agony and died a slow, tortuous death.

For now poison oozed from the frog's body, slime harmless to him but fatal to whatever living creature he touched. It became an ashé passed on through his generations, and his descendants were free to sing and croak all they wanted while the snakes kept their distance.

So afraid were the snakes that they never ate another frog, no matter how loudly they croaked.

The Birth of Red Blood Cells
From the Odu Osá Meji (9-9)

*As long as there is sound in the chest
there is life in the body.*

In the darkness stood sixteen clay statues, their lifeless eyes staring out over an ocean that thundered and crashed against the shore. The moon hung low over the surf, its reflection in the water creating a silvery path into the horizon, the place where water and sky met; it was the place where Olódumare's spirit slipped from heaven and made his way to earth followed by two of his odu—Ogundá and Odí. Before the statues the odu took form and their shapes were similar to that of the sculptures molded by Obatalá's hands. "He made them to look like us," said Ogundá, touching the machete that hung at his side. "He used his blade to carve them in our image."

Ogundá and Odí looked around and saw Obatalá sleeping peacefully, his back against the trunk of a coconut palm. They smiled at each other. Ogundá looked at Odí and said, "It is such a shame. Obatalá does all this work; he labors and creates the human form under the hot summer sun. And still, he doesn't get to see the mystery of life." Gently he touched the head of each figure, and then he blew on them one by one. Three spirits came to earth with Ogundá that day: Olori (the spirit enlivening the head), Ipari (the spirit enlivening the limbs), and Ipejeun (the spirit governing the internal organs). All three spirits settled in those sixteen forms; they took up residence in their heads and gave them the power of consciousness. "Now, they are complete."

"Not quite," said Odí. She understood the material world evolving before them in ways only a woman of her nature could; and gently she touched them in the place where the legs met the trunk. On some she touched the chest and sighed. "They are all exactly alike and they need to be different." Ogundá watched as half the figures became male, their loins bulging with strength, and half the figures became female, their chests swelling. "Now, they are complete."

"Should we not wait for Osá and the spirits she brings?" asked Olódumare. Incorporeal as he was, his voice seemed to come from everywhere at once—from the earth, from the sea, from the air—and the two odu shivered. His voice was the voice of nature.

"She is late, as she always is," said Odí. "The gifts we bring to these are enough."

"They have all they need," agreed Ogundá. "All they need to live is here except the breath of life."

Olódumare's essence strengthened around the sixteen figures; the night became thick and powerful around their forms. The two odu caught their breaths as the humans' chests rose for the first time, and light came to their eyes, the light of consciousness. They were alive.

Yet the figures stood still and did not move.

"Why do they not move?" asked Ogundá. "They have orí. They have consciousness."

"Why do they not move?" asked Odí. "They are male and female yet they do not move."

"Perhaps," said Olódumare, "we should have waited for Osá." The two odu looked childishly at their feet. They had been taught a lesson, but gently.

It was then that Osá slipped from heaven and crossed the silvery path to land. She was the last to arrive and there were tears in her eyes when she saw the world's first humans facing the sea. The moon had risen higher in the sky and their soft, black faces were bathed in its light. Their chests rose and fell in time with the crashing waves. She touched their bodies; they were firm and supple, but they were cold, cold like the sea and the night air around them.

Odí and Ogundá stood with their arms crossed watching Osá as she inspected the still, unmoving forms. "As always you are late," said Odí.

"We were here with Olódumare when he gave them breath. Where were you?"

"I was preparing the gift I bring." One by one Osá moved among the figures, touching them and kissing them lightly on their cheeks. "They have no heat. They have no passion. They have no fire in their veins. They cannot live like this."

Olódumare smiled at Osá. "What did you bring?"

"This." She conjured the spirit named Ejé Oruko Bale, and sent the spirit into the sixteen breathing forms. Cold flesh became warm and supple; gently they swayed and stretched and moved on the shore. For the spirit Osá birthed became the blood that flowed through the veins; it was red and hot, and gave warmth to the cold bodies. Ejé Oruko Bale was the essence of life and as long as it flowed, as long as there was the sound of a heart beating inside the chest, there was life and movement in the body.

"This," said Olódumare, "is the essence of life. Blood is the life. It is that which flows and nourishes all the spirits living in the human form; it is that which carries my ashé throughout each living creature."

Since that time blood has been the vehicle for life; it is the blood that ties all the spirits of the body together, and it is the loss of the blood that sets them all free to return to the spiritual world. And just as blood bound the gifts of Odí and Ogundá in the human form, so is Osá the tie that binds all three odu together and we say, "Where we see one—Ogundá, Odí, or Osá—we must consider all three."

This was the decree of Olódumare that day, and since that time Osá has followed Odí, and Odí has followed Ogundá; and no matter how slow any are in coming, they wait for each other before acting.

How the Turtle Won the Race
From the Odu Osá Ofún (9-10)

It takes speed and intelligence to win a race.

"I am the fastest creature who has ever lived!" said the dog as he ran down the road. He dashed past four turtles who sat in a tomato patch, nibbling on tomatoes under a hot summer sun. "I am surely much faster than any of you!" He laughed, turning back to run around them several times. "See? I can run circles around you!" Then the dog sped off leaving the turtles choking in his dust.

"I am sick of that dog," said one of the turtles, red juices dripping down the side of his mouth.

"I am sick of him, too," said another. "All he ever does is brag."

"He thinks he's the fastest creature in the world." The third turtle lifted his head and watched the dog disappear around a bend in the road.

When the dog was long gone, the fourth turtle said, "Maybe we should challenge him to a race?"

"A race?" they all asked at once.

"Yes, a race. Sometimes it takes craft and cunning to win a race, not speed. We can do it if we work together."

The three turtles listened to him as he spoke. They smiled; his plan was a good one.

Later that evening the challenge went out: the turtle wanted to race the dog. The dog barked and howled with glee when it reached his ears, and lightning-quick he ran to find that turtle foolish enough to race him. He found him surrounded by all three of his friends.

"You?" asked the dog. "You want to challenge me to a race?"

"I do," said the turtle. "I want to race you. And I will win."

The dog laughed so hard he almost fell over. "So be it. Tomorrow at sunrise we will race. How far shall we race, turtle?"

"From here to Oyó!" he said. Everyone gasped.

"That is many miles. Are you sure you're up to it?"

"Oh, I'm sure," said the turtle. "Of that you can be certain."

"Then sunrise tomorrow we will race." With a snicker he added, "And may the best . . . animal . . . win."

Their plan was simple: It involved all four of them and three chickens. In darkness, the first turtle walked slowly to the starting point while the other three each grabbed a raw chicken in their mouths and scattered to three points along the road to Oyó. When the sun rose the next morning, the dog found the turtle sleeping at the starting line, tucked away tightly inside his shell.

He rapped on the shell with his paw. "Wake up, turtle! It is time to race!"

Sleepily he poked his head out first, and then his four legs and tail. "Morning already?" he asked. "I am well-rested and ready to beat you, dog."

"We'll see about that. Are you ready?"

"I am!"

Before he took his first step the dog was off; and by the time the turtle had run only a few feet, the dog was out of sight. The turtle kept running, slow as he was, around the first bend of the road; and then, he walked into the bushes and slept. "My brothers will teach him to be humble," he thought as he drifted off to sleep.

After an hour of running the dog saw a dead chicken lying in the road. "What is this?" he thought, sniffing at its flesh. The smell was overwhelming and the dog took a single bite. Then he tore into the flesh. While he ate, the second turtle crept out of the bushes where he was resting; slowly, he ran toward the dog. "I am catching up with you, dog!" he called out.

The dog looked up. "How can this be?" he thought. "The turtle is too slow to make it this far this quickly." He looked at the chicken; his stomach rumbled. He looked at the turtle; he was gaining ground. The dog sighed and took off running again.

The turtle stopped and slept where he was.

After another hour of running the dog came across another dead chicken in the road. His belly rumbled; he stopped to eat. While he was growling and ripping into the flesh, the third turtle came out of the bush and began running toward the dog, slow as he was. With soft footsteps he ran right behind the dog and said, "Hello."

The dog jumped, a piece of meat still hanging in his mouth. He swallowed quickly. "How?" asked the dog. "How did you catch up with me? And how did you do it so quietly?"

"It doesn't matter *how*," said the turtle. "What matters is that I caught up with you again. I'm going to beat you at this race."

"Never!" He laughed and took off down the road to Oyó one more time. The turtle lay down and slept.

Again the dog ran for an hour; and again he saw another chicken lying in the road. By now he was ravenous. Teased by small bites of the previous two chickens and worn out from the constant running, the dog lay down to tear into the meat. He ate every last bit and even gnawed on the bones. When he was done he looked behind him; the turtle was nowhere to be seen. "He gave up!" said the dog, "and I will win the race!"

He picked up the last leg bone in his mouth—it was too tasty to leave lying on the road—and he ran toward Oyó again. In just minutes he was at the town's gates. There stood the turtle waiting for him. "How?" he cried out. "How were you able to get here first?" The bone still hung between his teeth.

The turtle smiled. "You were too intent on eating the chicken," he said, "and quietly I ran right by you!"

"You cheated!" cried the dog. "You cheated and now I will kill you!"

He growled deeply while the turtle trembled in fear; quickly, the turtle fled into the safety of his shell. The dog took a deep breath and dove for him—and the bone—the bone got sucked into his throat when he did. He fell on the ground gasping for air, but the bone stuck firm; and the dog died a slow, agonizing death while the turtle watched with glee.

"Never run with your mouth full!" the turtle said as the light went out in the dog's eyes.

No dog ever dared to race a turtle again.

Why Butterflies Stay in the Country
From the Odu Osá Ofún (9-10)

*Butterflies don't go to the city because
children will kill them.*

Butterflies are some of Olófin's most beautiful creatures; he made them as colorful and as delicate as any flower, but with wings, and they fly and flit through the forest more easily than petals ride the wind. Yet they weren't happy creatures. They knew that there was a world beyond theirs, and they wanted to see it, so they went to Olófin one day and told him, "We spent all our lives in the woods among the trees and the flowers and the animals. And we are bored. The world is a huge place, and we want to see what lies beyond the forest."

"But you are not creatures made for the civilized world," said Olófin. "You are creatures of the forest and there you are safe. Do not go to the cities. Stay away from the world of men. You will find only death there."

These were creature of impulse, however, and not creatures of great thought; so the next morning when the sun rose, hundreds of butterflies flitted through the forest and flew to the cities. The buildings were beautiful; the streets were incredible; and the air was filled with the most delicious smells. As they rested on the streets along came the children, and the insects watched these most curious creatures. Had they strong voices the streets would have been filled with their screams when little hands scooped them up; some of their wings were broken before they were tossed away carelessly to the wind while others died in rough, playful hands. Those who were not caught flew high above the children's heads and flew back to the forests, afraid for their lives.

The butterflies never went back to the cities, and that is why, today, we find them in forests and never on the streets.

Why the Sea Is Salty

From the Odu Osá Owani (9-11)

Everything has its consequences.

Sunrise: Osaguere stood on the shore gazing into the ocean's endless surf; it seemed angry today, rising and swelling with great waves that sent a fresh ocean mist over the beach. He watched the morning sun rise, looking not at the sun itself but at the path of bubbling sunlight over the water, a path that ended on the horizon where the sky touched the sea. It disappeared in the fresh, blue ocean and an even bluer sky, into a gentle, sloping curve that slipped from view. He licked his lips, tasting the ocean's mist on his skin. No water in the world tasted fresher than that from his mother, Yemayá. Gently he bent to scoop up a handful to drink before beginning his ebó.

Osaguere was a poor man and the ebó he offered that day was simple: on the sand he put seven green apples, seven green pears, and bunches of green grapes; and then he stood back and sang Yemayá's ancient songs as the waves reached out to the shore and sucked the offering into the sea. "I am but a poor man, Yemayá," he whispered into the waves when the last piece of fruit was sucked under the sea, "and I need help. The diviners said you would help me if I made ebó to you."

"I help all those who come to me with faith, and with ebó," said a woman's voice. Osaguere snapped around and froze; before him was one of the most beautiful women his eyes had ever seen. She was tall, imposing, with pendulous breasts meant for the suckling of babies and the tempting of men, and a waist so tiny it seemed at odds with the childbearing hips beneath them. Her face was dewy, rich, and black, and her eyes like dark pools of ink. Her hair was long and loose, coarse but kept in place with cowries and seashells woven into its strands. Osaguere's face was torn between astonishment and fear.

"Don't be afraid. You came here looking for me, but it was I who found you."

He threw himself to the sand, rolling from side-to-side before putting his head to the ground. Yemayá reached down and touched his shoulders gently, blessing him; and then with an almost preternatural strength helped him rise to his feet. They embraced, orisha and human, and Osaguere felt ashé like warm water flowing into his body. When they parted he reached out for her again; the feeling of separation was intense, like falling down a well. But Yemayá stood back and looked at him lovingly. He felt naked under her gaze.

"I live in more places than the sea, Osaguere. I've been watching you as you made ebó. I am most pleased. I've been listening to your singing. It brought joy to my heart. And now I have something for you."

She walked him to a palm tree that grew on the edge of the beach. Beside it sat a mortar; but Osaguere noted that it had strange markings up and down its sides. He stood close to Yemayá and even closer to the mortar, and something like a low-pitched hum seemed to fill his chest. "All your life you've lived in the shadow of your brother, Osamoni. All that is about to change."

Osamoni was Osaguere's older brother, and it was true—all his life he lived in his brother's shadow. Where Osamoni was brilliant Osaguere was dull; Osamoni was handsome and Osaguere was plain. His brother was favored by his parents while Osaguere was left to fend for himself in the world. And as the older brother, when their parents passed he inherited everything including the salt mines, and those mines were what made him wealthy beyond his wildest dreams. Osaguere remained poor.

"This is my gift to you, Osaguere." She looked at the stone mortar; it was slightly taller than his knees.

"I've seen these before but normally they are made of wood. This one is made of stone."

"Yes, stone. Stone taken deep from the earth. Stone that lies deep beneath your brother's salt mines. I mined the stone myself and with my own hands. My ocean runs beneath the earth in secret caves no mortal will ever see, and there is one that runs below your ancestral salt mines. I took the stone from which this mortar was carved from that place, and I carved it into a mortar with my own hands."

"Thank you, Yemayá." Osaguere looked at the mortar, puzzled. "But what am I to do with it?"

"Since the day your parents died I have watched over you, Osaguere. Even though your brother inherited the kingdom, and even though he got the salt mines, never once did you get bitter. You did your best with what you had. And today you came to make ebó. There was no bitterness in your heart. There was only love for me and hope for a brighter future."

"Still, what am I to do with the mortar?"

Yemayá smiled, ignoring his question. "Little did you know that your older brother stole everything from you. Your parents meant for you to have half their wealth. Your parents meant for you to have half the salt mines. They wrote everything down on a piece of paper; they gave specific directions as to how everything was to be divided equally. But your brother found that—he who was your own blood—he who was once your best friend. He destroyed that paper, and as the older brother he declared himself sole heir to all your parents owned."

"He would not do that!"

"He did. But this mortar sets all things right. This mortar has ashé and will make you a rich man."

Osaguere ran his hands over the mortar and felt . . . something. It was like the ashé that flowed to him from Yemayá, but not wet; it felt dry and warm and left a salty taste in his mouth.

"I taste salt," said Osaguere.

"Yes, that is the ashé of the mortar. Just as your brother amassed a fortune with the salt mines he stole from you, so shall you amass a fortune selling salt. The mortar will give it to you." She leaned in close to Osaguere. "Pay careful attention to what I teach you. Whenever you want salt, you say these words—'Dance, mortar, dance, and let the salt flow free!' Now, say it back to me."

Osaguere chanted the words and the mortar began to move, beating the earth. Each time it slammed into the ground a mound of salt appeared. Quickly the salt spread.

"And when you have enough salt," said Yemayá, "you say, 'Still, mortar, still, and let the salt be.' Now say it back to me."

He said the words—the mortar stopped. "That is amazing. I must write those words down."

"No!" said Yemayá. "The secret of the mortar is only for you. Never write down the words. One day you will be rich, and your brother will be poor, and you will be able to buy back the salt mines from him. One day you will be so rich that the kingdom will be yours. And when that happens there will be no need for the mortar anymore. I will take it back far beneath the earth for all time."

Osaguere thanked Yemayá for all she had given him, and with great difficulty he carried the heavy mortar back home.

His wife was waiting for him sullenly in the kitchen; she cooked over a stove by candlelight. When he walked in the kitchen she barely looked up. "It's late. What did the diviners tell you?"

He kissed her lightly on the cheek. "They told me I had to make ebó, and Yemayá would make me a rich man."

"The diviners always say that," she said. Her words were heavy, filled with grief. She turned to look at him. "And did you? Did you make ebó?" She saw the stone mortar he carried over his shoulders. He sat it down of the floor with a great thud. She jumped.

"I did. And I saw Yemayá today. She came to me. She gave me this."

"You saw Yemayá?" Her voice was thin and wispy. "In a dream? A vision? How did you see her?"

"She came to me and gave me this."

His wife smiled. Her husband had always been a dreamer given to tall tales about the orishas. "And what is *this*?"

"A salt mortar. Watch."

Softly Osaguere chanted the words Yemayá taught him; his voice was soft and unsure at first, but as he remembered the words his voice grew stronger. The mortar twitched and then jumped. His wife jumped as well when it landed on the floor with a great crash and lifted again. Beneath it was a mound of salt.

Osaguere stopped singing. Again and again the mortar lifted and slammed into the floor as if moved by unseen hands and the mound of salt spread and grew. Soon the entire floor was covered in salt. His wife stood there with her mouth open not moving, watching the salt grow around her feet.

"How?" she asked. "How do you make it stop?"

Again Osaguere chanted, only this time he spoke the words Yemayá taught him to make the mortar sit still. The mound of salt beneath it stopped growing and spreading. "We will be rich, my wife. We will sell our salt and be as rich as my brother."

She flew into his arms.

When word reached Osamoni that his brother was now a vender of salt, at first he did not believe it. But when his palace guards verified that Osaguere was, indeed, selling salt in the marketplace he was perturbed.

"My brother sells salt? Where does he get it from?"

"We don't know," answered his guard. He and his wife hawk it in the market and when they run out they return home. A few hours later they return, their cart overflowing with bags of salt; and they sell it cheaply."

"But they have no mines. They have no laborers. Where do they get it from?"

The guard was silent.

"Find out!" he said. "Watch my brother in the marketplace and when he runs out of salt, follow him. See where he gets it. See who he gets it from. I want to know . . . everything."

The guard did just that.

He returned later in the afternoon. Osamoni was waiting for him.

"What did you find out?"

The guard was pale-face when he told him, "It's magic."

"It's what?" Osamoni's face was twisted in disbelief.

"It's magic. Your brother has a stone mortar that he speaks to. It pounds the earth and salt comes . . . from nowhere. He and his wife bag it up as the mortar makes it."

"That's impossible."

"I know it seems impossible, but I watched it with my own eyes. He spoke to the mortar as his wife stood beside him, and then the mortar started moving up and down. It pounded the floor hard before lifting again. And each time it hit the floor, under it a pile of salt grew. After he stopped chanting it kept pounding and the salt pile kept growing. I watched them bag it, more than they could keep up with! And then I ran here to tell you."

Osamoni was quiet. When he spoke his voice was thin. "My brother always believed in magic and tall tales. Since he was a young child he was devoted to the orisha Yemayá. He spent a lot of time with priests and diviners. Maybe there is something to all that after all?" He looked at his guard sternly. "You remember these words he spoke?"

"I do." He spoke the words Osaguere said to the mortar. Osamoni held his hand up.

"Stop. That is enough. I want you to get that mortar for me tonight while my brother and his wife sleeps. Bring it to my ship. We'll set sail you and I. We'll travel just away from land and I'll test this mortar for myself. If it works . . . you get to live."

"Yes sir," said the guard before slipping away timidly.

"A magic stone mortar. Who ever heard of such a thing?" Osamoni asked himself.

While Osaguere and his wife slept, the guard slipped in quietly through the front door. It was locked, but the guard knew how to pick locks and in a few minutes he was in. His fellow guards stood just outside keeping watch. He made his way to the kitchen where the mortar sat still; and with a great effort, he lifted the heavy stone over his shoulders. As quietly as he came in he left; together with his men he made his way to port.

Osamoni was waiting on the ship.

By moonlight they set sail, following the stars just over the horizon's bend where there was no hope of anyone seeing what they were about to do. Osamoni looked back at the shore, its sandy beach glowing with the silvery sheen of the moon; he watched as it seemed to slip from view, swallowed up by the ocean. The stone mortar sat on the ship's deck; it, too, glowed in the moonlight, the hard white stone reflecting it like a thick star.

"You remember the words?" he asked his guard.

He smiled and stood tall. All the ship's crew came to the deck to watch and listen. Softly at first, his voice unsure of the words he began chanting. The mortar twitched; it levitated slowly before crashing into the deck with a thud.

There was a mound of salt beneath it.

"Keep chanting!" ordered Osamoni.

Again and again the guard chanted: Again and again the mortar slammed into the deck. Each time there was twice the amount of salt sitting on the deck; it grew and slid across the floor until the crew's feet were buried beneath it. "Enough!" ordered Osamoni. "That is enough for now. Men—we set for the next port. Bag this salt. When we get closer we will make more . . . and we will be rich!" The thought of producing salt without labor gave Osamoni visions of gold bars and more dancing in his head.

The guard stopped chanting; the mortar, however, did not stop pounding.

"That's enough!" he told the guard. "Make it stop."

"But I stopped," said the guard. Each time the mortar pounded on the deck, twice the amount of salt appeared. It had reached the stairs to the lower deck and was spilling down below.

"How did my brother make it stop? Do what he did!"

"I never saw him make it stop," said the guard.

"What?"

The ship started to rock and roll under the weight of the salt. "We're sinking!" cried one of the crewmen. "Throw it overboard. Quickly!"

The guard reached for the mortar but as he grabbed it, it shook him off. Another crewman reached for the mortar, but it threw him off as well. Yet another tried to grab the mortar but it slammed down on his hand, crushing it.

The boat began to sink; and so far was it from shore than none were able to swim back safely. They all drowned that day.

The next evening Osaguere stood at the shore gazing across the ocean. His mortar was gone, stolen with no witnesses to the crime, but Osaguere knew—his brother was the thief. There was no other explanation. Earlier that morning bodies had washed up on the shore, the bodies of his crewmen; and his ship had set sail secretly the night before. Men up late on the docks said they saw his guard carrying a strange object covered in sheets; he strained under the weight so they knew it was heavy. They knew not what it was—Osaguere had told no one about the mortar. And now that his brother was gone all that his parents once had was his. Even without the mortar he was a rich man.

A light mist worked up by the crashing surf and endless ocean breeze sprayed his face; he licked his lips. The water was salty, not fresh. Osaguere sighed.

Since that day, the sea has been salty.

10

PATAKÍS FROM THE COMPOSITES OF OFÚN

How the Pigeon Was First Sacrificed

From the Odu Ofún Ogundá (10-3)

Evil souls are filled with remorse.

It was still early when Ará Onú went into the forest. A light morning mist rose from the earth, but thin rays of sunlight sliced through the woods' thick canopy, melting it before it could become fog. Dew dampened the ground, muffling each footstep save for the occasional snap of a twig underfoot. He struggled with a cage slung across his back. It was heavy, with dozens of white birds inside—chickens, roosters, and guinea hens. His muscles popped and strained with the weight. He walked deeper through the trees, past bubbling brooks and through thorny bushes until he stood before an ancient Iroko tree. At its roots he set down the cage with a thud; the animals bristled and squawked at the sudden drop. Then, once again, there was silence.

Ará Onú sang songs as ancient as the earth itself if not older, his voice a soft baritone that rose in both volume and pitch. One by one, with a quick flick of his wrists, he tore off the heads of the animals and let the blood pour on the tree's gnarled roots. He followed the blood with honey, and the honey with feathers, and gathered the bodies back into the cage to carry home for his family's evening meal. This was Ará Onú's daily ritual; at the feet of the Iroko, he came to feed all the spirits of heaven and even God himself. He did this before he himself would eat for the day.

He barely noticed the hundreds of gentle orbs that came down from the sky like rain, descending on the blood and the honey and the feathers. The orbs always came, gentle lights that were the spirits of heaven; but this time there was something different. Within the orbs the figure of an old black man took shape, a man dressed in robes so white they shimmered with the brilliance of a thousand stars. The air in the forest seemed thicker; it pulsed and pushed against Ará Onú, so filled with ashé it was. The old man stood there in the lights, smiling, and Ará Onú knew, for the first time, he stood face-to-face with Olófin.

Quickly, he threw himself on the earth in reverence: face down in the mud with the blood and the honey and the feathers. So great was the power in the forest that morning that he barely noticed the mess staining his clothes.

Gentle but strong hands touched his shoulders, "You are blessed, son. Arise." The two embraced, and for a moment Ará Onú felt love like warm water washing over him and into him. When Olófin broke the embrace he realized the old man's robes were unstained although his were a mess. Olófin smiled with his arms held out as if to display the clean, crisp whiteness of his robes as heaven's greatest miracle.

Then Olófin spoke gently, "For years you have served heaven faithfully. You have fed us again and again, remembering our names and our rituals, and never once have you asked for anything in return, Ará Onú."

He blushed and stammered, "Father, I have my health and my family and my farm. What more could I want?"

"Life is good, is it not?" Olófin asked, but it was more a statement than a question and Ará Onú stood with tears in his eyes, not answering. "It is good to be thankful for what one has, for there are always those worse off. Thankfulness for a good, decent life is the best ebó there is. But service such as yours deserves recognition. I have come to bless you with ashé."

Ará Onú was about to throw himself in reverence again when Olófin reached out to stop him. "Your humility touches me, Ará Onú, so to you I give a gift. You are a farmer, the caretaker of the earth and the animals that walk its face. From now on, you will understand their speech. From the smallest worm to the greatest elephant, and of all animals great and small, you will understand the things they say." Gently, Olófin touched Ará Onú's ears, and suddenly the animal sounds in the forest sounded like words and speech; and he heard what they said as naturally as the language of any human.

"And what can I give you, Olófin? What can I do to honor you for this gift?" Tears spilled from his eyes as his mind wandered away from Olófin and toward the speech of the animals. They spoke of secret things to which no mortal man was ever privy.

Olófin smiled. "You are a wonderful man, Ará Onú. There are two things you can do. First, never tell anyone you can understand the speech of animals. What you hear is for your knowledge only. Second, I want you to raise a coop of white pigeons and doves in my honor. They are my favorite birds. They are humble birds, without an evil bone in them. They deserve your sweetness and your gentleness. That, son, will make me happy."

The sunlight in the forest brightened gently, and the heat rose as the sun climbed and bore down on the forest; Olófin stood back in a ray of sunlight, and gently his form melted. For what seemed like hours, Ará Onú sat there listening to the sounds of the forest. And then, he gathered up his cage and walked home.

For years Ará Onú kept his secret: he knew the speech of animals, but never told anyone what he heard. Stories of sun and moon, sky and earth, even the secrets of his neighbors, or kings and queens in far away towns—all these things he knew by listening to them speak. In honor of Olófin, the farmer kept a coop of white pigeons and doves, animals he raised in honor of the mighty one. And although he kept up his morning ritual of feeding Olófin and all of heaven's spirits at the roots of the Iroko, never once did he touch the pigeons or offer them in sacrifice.

He did this so Olófin would never be offended, or take back his gift.

In time Olófin blessed Ará Onú with yet another gift; as the number of pigeons in his care grew, so did his riches swell, and if their numbers ever dwindled, so did his blessings. Of all the animals on his farm, the pigeons and doves became the most pampered, a fact that was not lost to them.

He was tending to his chickens one morning, throwing grain on the muddy earth when he overheard the birds gloating, "We are Ará Onú's favored birds! See how he scatters grains on the earth for the common chickens and roosters, but for us, we eat from clean bowls. We never need put our beaks to the mud."

One of the hens stopped pecking at the earth and looked up at the coop. It was lined with clean straw. She looked back at her own henhouse, and saw that her dung was slung throughout.

"That's right," said another pigeon. "We sleep on clean straw. You sleep in your own excrement. We are loved, and pampered. And no one bothers us."

"No one at all!" said another white dove. "All of Ará Onú's house feasts on your flesh. You chickens are stupid, really. You see him carry off your mothers and your fathers and your children, yet you never question why they never come back. It is because he eats you."

"Yes. He EATS you!" The pigeon flapped her wings and laughed an evil laugh while all the roosters and hens stopped eating. They gathered in a tight group and shook with fright as they watched the farmer spread their grain. "He's fattening you up!" mocked the pigeon. "And when you are fat, you will feed him."

"But why?" screamed a cowering hen. "Why would he eat us, and not you?"

The oldest pigeon flew down from the coop and landed on its master's shoulders. Ará Onú smiled, not betraying that he understood every word the evil bird said. "It is because Olófin himself has blessed us! We are his favorite birds. But Olófin is an old man, and a lazy man at that, so he makes this stupid man care for us in his place. Ará Onú is nothing but Olófin's pawn, and he is more a slave to us than we are to him." Gently the bird nuzzled the farmer's hair, and he lifted a hand to which the dove jumped. Carefully, he put the dove back in the cage. "See? He handles us with kid gloves. He is afraid to hurt us!"

Late that night, Ará Onú walked empty-handed to the ancient Iroko. He knelt at its roots and put his head to the earth. The only light was that of a pale, crescent moon; and the forest seemed filled with shadows. The animals whispered in darkness, but so faint was their speech that Ará Onú understood not a word of it. He cared not for the secrets of animals—he only wanted to pray to Olófin, and hoped he heard.

"Father," he whispered against the roots of the tree, his voice a faint echo in the forest. "Once you told me that the white pigeons and doves were among the most humble creatures. But they aren't so humble anymore." He looked up at the tree towering above him; he saw the crescent moon faintly through its branches. "They torment the other birds on the farm. I tried to be humane when I make sacrifice. I bring the birds away, to you and all of heaven, and never do I let any see the demise of their kind. But now they know. They know because the pigeons torment them."

A hand so gentle it felt like the brush of a branch on Ará Onú's back made him stiffen; and when the hand tightened its grip on his shoulder, he cried out. Quickly he turned, falling back against the tree. He saw Olófin's figure standing above him. "Surprised? I walk the earth all hours of the day and night. The night is so peaceful."

Ará Onú scrambled first to his feet, and then remembering his manners, he prostrated himself to Olófin. The orisha blessed him and bid him to rise. They embraced.

"Then you know why I came. You heard?"

"Yes, Ará Onú, I knew before you told me. I know everything that happens in this world." Olófin made a deep sigh. "It is because of my love for them that they lived such pampered lives. And it was for their purity and humility that I loved them. But their purity has become vanity, and their humility pride. Now I feel no love for them. And you were neither their slave nor mine. I think that accusation is what bothers me the most. So now, treat them equal to the other beasts on your farm. Make them a part of your daily sacrifices to the dead in heaven, and to me. Let the sacred Iroko feed on their life-blood."

Ará Onú agreed, and watched Olófin walk sadly through the woods.

The next morning, Ará Onú came to the barn with his cage to select the animals for that day's sacrifices. All the roosters and chickens saw him coming, and instead of walking around him fearlessly they cowered at the back of the barn. Ará Onú smiled; and with that smile on his face he walked outside to the pigeons' coop instead. When they saw Ará Onú approach, they had no fear. Instead, when he put his hands inside the cage they jumped on his arms willingly, and when he put them inside the smaller cage they had no fear.

As Ará Onú walked away from the coop and the hens started to spread out, the pigeons taunted, "Don't worry. He'll be back for you soon!"

When the pigeons realized their fate it was too late. In the most solemn of ceremonies, Ará Onú offered them one by one to Olófin; and he let their brothers and sisters watch in horror. For their vanity and pride, they became a sacrificial bird; and because Ará Onú was faithful to heaven, Olófin continued to make him prosperous on the earth in spite of the pigeon's dwindling numbers. Never again were the pigeons and doves safe from sacrifice, and in time, they became the favored food of most of the orishas.

The moral of the story is simple: be neither vain nor proud, for in the eyes of the orishas, there is no one on earth or in heaven who is not above punishment for their transgressions.

Why Orúnmila Eats Hens, and Not Roosters

From the Odu Ofún Irosun (10-4)

*Graciousness begets graciousness, but evil
brings more of the same.*

For most of his life Orúnmila lived in the town called Ilé Ifé; but he was bored, and one day he decided to see the world. So he packed his bags and mounted his horse, and alone he left to see the world. In his hand he had a map, and that served as his guide.

City-to-city he rode along the well-traveled road, but each place seemed as boring as the one previous to it. After days of riding he came to a fork, and one path seemed less traveled. He checked his map— it was not there. Orúnmila took a deep breath and guided his steed down the unworn, unmapped road. After a half-day's travel he came to a small town, a village named Mono. At its gate was a strange-looking, short man covered in hair. Orúnmila slid from his horse and greeted the stranger, asking him, "I am traveling from Ilé Ife, and have never seen this town before. What is its name?"

"The town is called Mono," said the young man. His accent was strange, but still the orisha understood his words.

"And my name is Orúnmila," the orisha said. "I am pleased to meet you. What is your name?"

"My name is Mono," he said.

Orúnmila scratched his head. In the town of Mono was a young man named Mono. It seemed bizarre, but not too farfetched. To make conversation, he asked, "You seem quite young? Where are your parents? What is your father's name?'

"My parents are at home, and my father's name is Mono," said the boy.

Orúnmila smiled. It was a strange smile; he was in the town of Mono talking to a boy named Mono, whose father was named Mono. "And your mother? What is her name?"

"Her name is Mona," the boy said.

He couldn't take it. "This is the town of Mono and your name is Mono. Your father's name is Mono, and your mother is Mona? Do you have any brothers or sisters?"

"Yes, I have an older brother named Mono, an older sister named Mona, a younger brother named Monito and two younger sisters named Monita!"

Not liking this, but not wanting to be rude, Orúnmila said, "Thank you for speaking with me, Mono, but I don't think I like this town. I am going to keep riding. Have a nice day."

"You, too," said Mono, and he watched as Orúnmila left.

Orúnmila rode his horse until he came to a new town alongside the unmapped road; there was a sign by the front gate that said Elefante. "This is a strange name for a town!" Orúnmila said to himself, and he slid down from his horse and walked it past the city gates. In time, he found a strange-looking young girl playing in the streets.

"Hello," said the orisha. "My name is Orúnmila. There is a sign outside the front gates that says Elefante. Is this the town's name?"

"Why, yes it is!" said the little girl, who stopped playing her game and looked at the orisha kindly. "And my name is Elefanta," she said.

He gave a disturbed grin, but the young girl only smiled. "And what is your mother's name?" he asked, afraid of the answer.

"Elefanta!" she said, still smiling.

"And would your father's name be . . . Elefante?" Orúnmila asked, not wanting to hear the answer.

"Yes!" the young girl said. "How did you know?"

"It was a good guess," said Orúnmila, rubbing the girl's head. "Have a nice day. I must continue my travels."

As he mounted his horse, the young girl went back to playing her game.

As the days turned to weeks, Orúnmila came to many new lands. There was the village of Perros, where everyone had the name Perro or Perra; there was the land of Ratos, where everyone had the name Rato or Rata; but, finally, Orúnmila came to the town of Gallina, and the place seemed different. He stopped to speak to a young girl who was walking casually in the street.

"I am tired," he said to her, "and I am afraid I am quite lost. My name is Orúnmila. What is yours?" The orisha had a weary smile on his face, and the young girl looked at him curiously.

"My name is Pollita!" she said, and she held an animal skin bag up to him. "You look thirsty. Would you like some water?"

Orúnmila took a great drink before speaking again. "So, you are Pollita, and this is the town of Gallina?"

"Yes, it is," she said. "Where are you from, sir?"

"Ilé Ifé. I've been traveling for weeks, looking for someplace new to settle. It is beautiful here. Can I ask you . . . what is your father's name?"

He held his breath until the girl answered, "Gallo!" And then he smiled. He was happy, for this was the first town in which people seemed to have different names.

"And your mother? What is her name?"

"Gallina," said the girl.

"Pollita, I have traveled far, and I am weary. Would you take me to your house so I could speak to your parents?" And Pollita led Orúnmila to her home.

When Orúnmila arrived at Pollita's house he saluted Gallina and explained who he was. "My good lady," he said, "I am the orisha known as Orúnmila, and I am weary from my travels. Please let me stay here a bit in your fine home, and rest."

Gallina looked sternly at her daughter, and then warily at Orúnmila as she said, "You may be who you say that you are, but my husband is not home; and when he is not here I do not accept male guests in the house, not chaperoned as I am. You may not come inside, nor may you stay near my land. Leave me in peace now!" she demanded. Orúnmila was exhausted, and now he was angered. Without saying goodbye to Gallina, he turned to Pollita and bade her farewell. Then, slowly, he left.

Orúnmila strode his horse, riding off angrily. After a short while he saw a strange man walking the way from which he had come, and again, he slid off his horse and greeted the stranger. "I am Orúnmila," he said, "and I have traveled far from Ilé Ifé, looking for a new land in which to settle."

"Welcome to the town Gallina," said the man pleasantly enough. "You will find that our town is as good a place as any to settle."

"Yes," said Orúnmila, "but not everyone is as friendly as you. I met a woman named Gallina, and she all but threw me off her land."

The man looked disturbed, and looked back in the direction from which Orúnmila had ridden. "Gallina would be my wife. I am Gallo. And I am sorry for her inhospitable nature. She is not too trusting. But, please, it would make me happy if you would come back to my home and rest, and have dinner with us tonight."

The orisha accepted Gallo's invitation; together on Orúnmila's horse, they rode back to Gallo's house. Gallina saw her husband and the stranger approaching, and her voice was shrill when she said, "Not just this afternoon I threw this man out of my house and off my property. How dare you bring him home!" Her voice sounded like little more than an angry cluck, but Orúnmila, who knew all the languages of the world, understood every word she said.

As the two men slid off the horse Orúnmila told Gallo, "Your wife has insulted me not once but twice today and I am no ordinary man. I am Orúnmila, an orisha, one who deserves respect. I will stay in your home as you have offered, but only as long as I am not alone with this miserable woman."

Gallo hung his head in shame; in front of an orisha, he had been embarrassed, but he understood. And every morning after that, when Gallo left to work in the fields, Orúnmila left as well.

Never once did Gallina make Orúnmila feel welcome, and as the days passed, he discovered that her true nature was one of bitterness.

The morning came when Gallina had enough of her unwanted visitor, and while he dressed in the guest's bedroom, an argument broke out between husband and wife. In anger, the orisha listened.

"I cannot take another day of that man!" she wailed. "Every day I have to cook for him and clean up after him, and at night when he comes home with you, we have no privacy. This is our family's home. Not a motel."

"He is an orisha," Gallo said, "but more importantly, he is my guest. I will have him as long as he wishes to stay."

"I want that man out!" she screamed, and she began to peck at her husband. "I want him out, and I want him out now!"

Gallo, not knowing what else to do, let his wife peck him out of his own house; and once they were in the front yard, she turned and kicked dust in his face.

Orúnmila stood on the front porch. Inside the house he had peeked from his room to see Gallina pecking at her husband, and now that he saw her kicking dust in his face, he got angry. In a movement as swift as the wind, he bored down on the vile hen, grabbing her by the legs and holding her upside down at his waist. Gallo's beak dropped open.

"Gallo!" he said, "You will always be treated as one of my best friends for you alone treated me well in this house, but your wife knows no respect—not to you, her husband, and not to me, an orisha. She needs to learn a lesson!"

It was there, in front of her own husband, that the hen became the favored sacrifice of Orúnmila; and it is for that reason that even today, Orúnmila will eat hen, but never a rooster.

Ananagú: How Osogbo Was Freed in the World

From the Odu Ofún Oché (10-5)

You can have everything, and lose it all
in the blink of an eye.

The young woman lay sweating beneath her sheet; the bed was soaked; fever licked at her skin, eating its color and making her look waxen. Her breathing came in rapid bursts before stopping, and then, to catch her breath again she gasped at the air like a landlocked fish. Ofún stood over her, stooped over partly with age but mostly with concern, examining her.

He knew the woman was dying. He also knew he could save her for there was no candle burning at her feet.

He called to the woman's young daughter, the only other person in the house. She was only eight years old. She came, her face wrinkled with confusion. "Is mommy okay?" It was a doll-baby voice, stressed and on the verge of sobbing.

"No, little girl, mommy is not okay. But she will be. I need you to run outside to my horse. There is a bag hanging on his side. Do you like horses?"

"Yes," she said, not taking her eyes off her mother.

"Good. My horse likes little girls; so don't let him frighten you. Just go get that bag for me. It's hanging over his side, on a rope. Do you think you can do that? I don't want to leave your mommy alone."

She nodded, and backed out of the room. Ofún put one of his hands on the woman's head, and another one on her belly. He started to chant. He chanted and prayed until the little girl came back with two bags, one in each hand. "I forgot," he smiled, "that there were two. Thank you for bringing them both. Now, can you go wait outside while I try to heal your mommy?"

She ran out without a word.

Ofún pulled a white bolt of fabric and some herbs from one of his bags; he covered the woman's feverish body with the cloth. She trembled with delirium, but the cloth seemed to move with more than just her shaking. It boiled and rippled with an unseen force. He passed handfuls of the herbs over her body while he chanted an ancient incantation; the sheet vibrated and moved violently. Bit by bit, he scattered the leaves on the white sheet, and slowly, he rolled it into a tight cylinder, folding it over itself several times until it was a tight ball. This he tied with a length of cord.

The fever broke; the woman's breathing returned to normal. Ofún sighed, and smiled.

The ball he held in his hands shook angrily. "Another of the world's evils trapped," he whispered to himself as he stuffed it back into his bag. He latched it firmly. The bag seemed to tremble. "I'm getting too old for this," he said.

For Ofún was an old man. Many decades before, while he was still young, his godmother Ikú shared a great secret with him in return for a pact; Ikú had taken Ofún deep into the woods, to the roots of an ancient Iroko tree. It was midnight, and their only light was that of a moon that loomed low and full over the trees. There, at the Iroko's feet, she had told him, "This was the first one of its kind. When the orishas themselves came down to earth, they climbed down the branches of this ancient tree. When I first came to be, it was here, with this Iroko as witness, that I first drew form. And it is here that I make my pact with you."

"What pact?" Ofún had asked her. There was no fear, only curiosity.

"The pact with which I give you power over death itself!" Her voice had been strong, full, echoing through the forest. Dark birds took flight as her words shook the branches in which they slept. In her hands she held out a branch covered with leaves, and carefully, Ofún took it from her. "This is the one herb that has power over me, and over all death.

Remember it well. It grows sparsely throughout the forest, but with your keen eyes you will find it wherever you go. Just look for the oldest Iroko tree you can find, and there, you will find this."

"And what am I to do with this?" Ofún had asked, holding the leaves to his nose so he could smell their woodsy scent.

"Whenever you are called to heal the sick, if they respond to no other treatment, they will respond to this. Clean those for whom all hope is lost with this herb and all sickness will flee their bodies."

"And I can save anyone?"

"You can save almost anyone, but not everyone. Before you clean a patient with this herb, look at his feet; if with your eyes you see a candle burning there, a candle that no one else but you can see, do not clean him. That person's life belongs to me, and you must allow me to take it."

Ofún had smiled. "I accept our pact, godmother."

There were days Ofún wished he had not accepted that pact, days when the work was draining, and his body seemed not to have the strength to heal. Today was one of those days. Ofún touched the young woman's forehead, and he looked at the bag that seemed to jerk and twitch of its own accord. Since the day he made that pact with his godmother Ikú, it had not been enough for Ofún to heal the dying; no, he wanted to heal the world and free it from all misfortune. Since the herb made healing easy enough, he turned to the study of magic and sorcery, and learned how to trap the spirit of the diseases from which he saved the human body. All these ills he kept locked up in a special room in his house, a room, which no one but he was allowed into. Yet osogbo was a powerful family of spirits, and each one he trapped drained away a bit of his own health and resolve.

"Still, it is work worth doing," he said to himself.

The young woman's eyes fluttered open. They looked glazed with confusion. "Who are you?"

"I am the physician your neighbors sent for. My name is Ofún."

She managed a weak smile. "Where is my daughter?" Ofún called for her.

By nightfall, the young mother's strength returned. She sat in a chair holding her daughter, Ananagú, in her lap, stroking her hair carefully with her hand. Ofún sat across from them and smiled against the strained silence. Finally, the young woman spoke, "I was afraid today, and I need to thank you."

"You are welcome, of course," said Ofún. "It is a doctor's duty to tend to the sick."

"Please," she paused and took a deep breath. "Let me finish." She waited for Ofún to nod his head slightly. "I was afraid today, not for myself, but for my daughter, Ananagú. I thought I was dying, and I have no husband. I have no relatives. Thank Olófin I have good neighbors with sense enough to send for you, but as you saw, while I lay in my sickbed, Ananagú was all alone. If I had died, she would be alone."

"But you are alive and well!" Ofún said. "And your daughter is not alone."

"She might have been had you not come in time. And it is for this reason that I am asking you to do me, us, and her, a great honor."

Ofún's eyes narrowed a bit. "What honor would you have me give you? I am just a simple country doctor."

She took a deep breath before speaking. "I would like you to stand as godfather to my daughter. No one lives forever. I could have died today. It is only because of you that I did not. But had I died, she has no one. If you would be her godfather, my mind would be at peace knowing that if something happened to me, she would have you."

Tears welled up in Ofún's eyes. When he was a young man he had a wife who died, and he had a daughter with that wife, a daughter who died just days before her wedding and whose body later disappeared, stolen, so he believed, by evil spirits. Perhaps the same evil spirits that he spent his life trapping. Gently he wiped at his eyes with his fingertips, and blinked rapidly to clear them. He smiled. "I would be honored to be Ananagú's godfather," he said. "Truly, honored."

Before he could say another word, the young girl flew off her mother's lap and embraced him. Both the mother and the old man cried freely.

When Ofún was not tending the sick, he was spoiling his goddaughter; the years passed until she was a young woman, hauntingly beautiful, with eyes that resembled those of the daughter he lost decades before. Those eyes made him love her more deeply; it was more like the love of a father for a child, not that of a godfather for his charge. Ananagú returned his love unashamedly, and so close were they that most of the villagers thought they were father and daughter. The young mother, not so young anymore, loved Ofún as well for all he did for her child. It was as deep as any family bond that ever existed on the earth.

One day, Ananagú's mother came to Ofún; her face was sorrowful, and he invited her into his house. "You look troubled. What is bothering you?" Ofún asked. She looked away, a single tear in her eye. "Please," he said, taking her chin gently in his hand, and with a handkerchief, he wiped the tears from her eyes. "Tell me what is wrong?"

"I can't find work anywhere in town. Things are really bad right now. I think that if I travel, I can find work; but a life lived on the road is no life for Ananagú. She has friends here. And her teachers are here. And you are here." Her voice trailed off.

"Yes, I am here for her. I was blessed when you named me her godfather." Ofún saw the sorrow clouding the woman's face, and it broke his heart. "How can I help? You know I have many charms."

"No, I don't need charms. Nor do I need witchcraft. I need work. And while I am away, working, I was hoping that Ananagú could stay with you. She loves you. She'd be happy here for a time."

Ofún smiled. He loved Ananagú as if she were his own daughter, and only Olófin knew how much he missed her when she was away. "I would love to have her stay with me. While you are away I will care for her as if she were my own flesh and blood. No harm will come to her."

The tears came from the woman's face as her arms encircled Ofún tightly; he felt the love and gratitude flowing into him as if it were the most powerful ashé. "You are such a good man, Ofún. I love you, too, as if you were my own father."

Ofún cried as well.

❋

It was a sad day when Ananagú's mother left her at Ofún's house. Ananagú cried; her mother cried, and Ofún cried. "You be good and listen to Ofún," she said, her hand caressing Ananagú's head. "And I won't be gone too long. There's no work here, and we are broke. The only way I can provide for you is if I travel to find work. When I am settled again, I will come back for you."

The mother's face twisted as she tried to hold back her tears; but the tears came. They were hot and salty, and left red streaks down her face. "I love you so much."

"I love you, too. I'll miss you." Ananagú wiped away her own tears and turned to Ofún; she smiled. "But I'll be fine. My godfather will take good care of me."

"You're such a good girl," her mother said. The three embraced one final time before parting, and Ananagú stood at Ofún's side, his hand on her shoulder, while they waved. When her mother was gone, Ofún looked down at Ananagú. "We should go inside and chat. While you are here, there will be rules."

"Aren't there always?" She smiled.

They were having lunch when Ofún gave Ananagú the rules she was to live by in his house. She listened intently.

"You know that I am a priest, and I deal heavily in the spiritual world."

"Yes, godfather. I know."

"And you know that I am a doctor and I heal the sick."

"I know that as well," she said.

"For years I have advised your mother, and since you were but a toddler, I have taken care of you spiritually, and have taught you the ways of our orishas."

Ananagú smiled. "Yes, godfather, you have. But what has this to do with the rules?"

"To the point," he thought to himself. "Just like me." Then, he addressed his goddaughter. "Ananagú, in this world are some terrible things, and I have spent my life studying those terrible things. I have dedicated my life to healing. Along the way, I have come across some things that are . . . not for the eyes of children. Nor are they for the eyes of those who are not initiated into the mysteries of the orishas. You have full run of my house, but there will always be two rooms that are off-limits to you."

Ananagú's eyes sparkled at the hint of mystery. "What rooms might those be?" She listened intently. Children always wanted to know about what they were not supposed to know.

"My chambers, of course, are off-limits. I am your godfather, not your real father, and it would be unseemly for you to be in there." She nodded her head in understanding. "But there is a room in this house where I keep all the tools of my work, spiritual tools, and that room is always locked. You must never, ever try to go in there. Do we understand each other?"

"Yes, godfather." She smiled innocently as she spoke. "I won't ever go in either room."

Ofún looked at her sternly. He was worried, but saw that she understood.

That night, Ofún was called away to tend someone who was sick. A frantic young man came beating on his door, and when Ofún answered it the man insisted, "My sister is very sick. You must come now."

"What is wrong with her?" he asked. Ananagú, who heard the commotion, stood behind her godfather and listened.

"She was bitten by a snake. Her leg is swollen. It's blue. And she just lays there; she's delirious and talks crazy talk. We think she's dying."

"Wait for me here," he said, inviting the young man inside his house.

Ananagú took him by the hand and led him to a chair while Ofún ran behind the door of the forbidden room. "Godfather has to gather his medicines. Please, sit. Relax. He won't be long."

The young man sat in the chair shaking. He jumped when Ofún

burst out of his room with bags in his hands. Ananagú shivered—she thought she heard a pained moan coming from the room behind her godfather.

"I am ready. Let's go." Together, Ofún and the young man walked off into the night.

Ananagú shut the front door behind them, and she was alone. For some time she stood at the front door listening; faint but awful sounds seemed to come from behind the forbidden door. Even there, by the front door of Ofún's house, she could hear them. They called to her. When she was sure her godfather and the man were long gone, quietly she crept across the room toward the door, that awful, mysterious door, and she put her ear to it. She listened.

Its wood felt warm, almost feverish, and it seemed to vibrate against her ear. She pressed the side of her face harder into it; the vibration tickled her skin and rattled her brain. Her breath was coming in short, rapid bursts and her heart pounded in her chest, but she barely noticed. She only listened to the whispers inside that room, whispers that seemed not of this world. "What does he have in there?" she thought.

"Ananagú . . ." One of the voices whispered her name. She sucked in her breath and jumped back from the vile door. Then there were a thousand whispers, all chanting her name in a cacophony that sent goose bumps down her skin.

She ran to her own room and hid under the covers of her bed. "What awful things does godfather have in that room?" she whispered to herself. Ananagú fell into an exhausted but fitful sleep.

When Ananagú woke up the next morning, Ofún was still away. Alone, she waited in the front room, sitting in a chair and staring at that door. There were still whispers, and they frightened her. Suddenly, they stopped, and almost immediately the front door opened. It was Ofún.

Ananagú knew he was exhausted; his hair was an uneven mass of tight curls, and it seemed a bit greyer than it had before he left the house last night. His clothes were wrinkled, and his old man's gait seemed a bit older. Under his arm was a bag. Something inside was moving, disturbing the fabric. With no more than a nod toward his goddaughter, Ofún unlocked that mysterious door and disappeared inside the room. When it seemed he had stayed inside too long, Ananagú was afraid, and slowly she walked to it. She knocked, but gently. She thought she heard Ofún chanting.

He came out visibly upset. "What have I told you about this door, Ananagú?"

"That what's inside it is not for my eyes."

Ofún pushed the door shut; and in his rush, he forgot to lock it. "That's right, young lady, what lies inside is not for your eyes. You are not to go near it."

"You never said that, godfather," Ananagú argued. "You never told me to not go near it. You told me to not go inside of it. And I was worried. Strange things happened while you were gone last night."

"What. Strange. Things?" Ofún emphasized each word separately, and his eyes narrowed with worry. "If you did not open this door or go inside this room, what strange things could have happened?"

"There were whispers after you left godfather. Awful, terrible whispers. I stood at the door and listened. And the voices know my name. They called out to me."

Ofún trembled where he stood. "This is not good, Ananagú. You should not be here, not if those things know your name. I will send a messenger for your mother, someone to bring her home. My work as a healer exposes me to some awful things, and you, a young lady, should not be around them."

"I want to stay," she argued, still eyeing the door. Watching her looking at that awful door sent chills down Ofún's back.

"No, you're not staying. Not now. I'm going into town to hire a messenger. He will go to your mother and tell her to come back for you." He saw tears in Ananagú's eyes. "It is for the best."

"I'm sorry, godfather. I didn't mean to make you angry." She hugged him tightly and cried.

"I'm not angry, child. I'm just worried. You should not be here around my work."

Ofún left the house. He left Ananagú alone while he went to hire a messenger to find her mother. Ananagú was alone, alone with the door, and the room, and the whispers.

What neither knew was this: Ananagú's mother missed her daughter terribly. She had already decided to come back home for her. Ofún's messenger would never reach her.

It was early evening and Ofún had not returned; Ananagú was alone, and the whispers were at it again. Sometimes they sounded like the rushing of a great wind, and other times they were gentle, like a breeze wafting through the forest. Always, they were sinister, and each time they called her name it made Ananagú shiver. But they brought no harm, and in time, Ananagú, almost feverish, got up from her chair and crept to the door. The closer she got the louder and more insistent the voices were, and when she could not help herself any longer, she reached out and touched the doorknob.

Immediately, there was silence.

"Hello?" she called out to the whispers. Again, only silence. The doorknob felt warm in her hands.

"It cannot hurt to take just a peek?" It was spoken as a fact, but in itself was a question. When no one answered, she turned the knob. Still, there was silence.

Gently, she opened the door. The room was dark, and it took her eyes a few moments to adjust to the darkness. "Hello?" her voice a whisper itself.

She shivered as her eyes adjusted to the twilight. A single lamp was lit, its flame burning low, but it was enough to see that the walls themselves were draped with white sheets, and on the floor were white sheets with bumps of various sizes beneath them. "Hello?" she whispered again. "Is anyone in here?"

She felt warm water washing down her legs when one of the sheets rose from the floor, but just a bit, and something seemed to turn beneath it. There was a weak whisper, "Ananagú? Is that you?" So soft was it she wondered if she imagined it. The sheet settled over what appeared to be the form of a woman; it stretched out, her hips and breasts pressed up under the flimsy cloth. She thought she could make out a face beneath the fabric. "Ananagú, help me," the voice pleaded.

She walked closer to the sheet. An arm rose beneath the fabric, reaching out for her. "Who are you?" Ananagú asked.

"Ofún has kept me prisoner here, Ananagú. He has kept many of us prisoner, against our will. We cannot escape. He is an evil man." One by one the sheets twisted and rose until Ananagú thought she could make out the forms of more women, men, and children all around her, bound beneath the sheets by something she could not see.

"My godfather Ofún is a good man. He is a doctor. He is a healer. He would not do such an evil thing."

"But he has," said the woman's voice again, tinged with sadness. "He keeps us locked up and when no one is around, he does terrible things to us. Things of which we cannot speak to one such as you."

"No!" she backed away.

"Yes! You cannot leave us here. You yourself are in danger now. You know his secret. And if you keep his secret, you will be just as guilty as he. Lift the sheets. See for yourself how he keeps us bound."

"It won't hurt. It won't hurt to look," Ananagú told herself. She knelt before the sheet covering the woman who spoke to her, and gently, she pulled at it. Some unseen force held it down.

"Pull harder," cried the woman. "It is bound with magic. And do it quickly. Ofún is coming back!"

Her palms were slick with sweat when she grabbed the sheet again, and with all her might she leaned back and pulled. There was a great tearing of fabric, and Ananagú fell back still holding the ripped cloth in her hand.

Ofún was at the front door when he heard the cloth shred; thunder rumbled, but not from outside. It came from the house. "Ananagú!"

he cried as he pulled at his door. It was stuck, and held fast.

He heard Ananagú scream. And Ofún himself jumped in fear when a woman's hand grabbed him and spun him around. "That was my daughter! What is happening?" she wailed.

Inside the house, Ananagú knew fear. With the shredding of one white sheet came a chain reaction, and all the white sheets in the room buckled and shredded as if ripped by knives; and instead of human figures, terrible shadows rose from beneath them. Such was her terror that Ananagú's hair turned white, and thousands of shadows rose up in the room. The windows shattered, and so thick were the shadows that escaped that the sky outside went dark.

It was then that Ananagú died in fright; and such was her fear that she looked like an old woman, a hag, when life left her body.

Ofún screamed in anger; and the front door cracked, splintered by the evil that escaped his house that day. He stood, frozen, while the mother ran inside. She ran to the forbidden room and saw the shredded white sheets, and the macabre implements of witchcraft and magic that lay beneath them. In the rubble, and in the darkness, she barely recognized the shell that was once her daughter.

"Ofún!" she screamed, tearing at her own hair. The old man came running to the room, and when he saw his goddaughter's lifeless body, he crumpled to the floor, a babbling idiot.

"Ofún, evil witch!" the mother cried. "You killed my daughter with your magic."

"No," he trembled on the floor.

"She is dead! And her lifeless body lays here amid all your tools of sorcery."

"No, no, no . . ." he cried. It was all he could say.

In agony, the mother lifted her daughter's lifeless body. "I never want to see you again. And I will tell everyone of the evil you brought to us this day."

It was there, with the disobedience of Ananagú and the carelessness of Ofún, that all the osogbos of the world were released in one great mass of anger and evil; and since that time, in return for their capture, they have plagued humans and the world with all their power.

Yet one osogbo was unable to escape; one remained trapped beneath the white sheets, and try as it did, it could not leave. That was hopelessness. It was the only thing that saved the world from utter destruction.

Still, Ofún died a miserable, lonely, and reviled man.

11
PATAKÍS FROM THE COMPOSITES OF OWANI

The Old Woman and the Leopard
From the Odu Owani Ogundá (11-3)

The leopard changed his clothes
so the hunters would not catch
him, but still, he fell in the trap.

Yewande's ancient bones screamed when she yanked on her door, trying to open it; a rope tied to the outside handle tethered it to a spike pounded deep in the earth, and it budged only a few inches. She pulled again but not as hard—her shoulder still ached from her first try. She pulled with both hands, pushing futilely against the doorframe with her left foot. Still it held fast, but the opening was enough for her to put one arm through and claw at the knot. Ekundayo, her son, tied that knot well, and no matter how hard she fumbled with it the rope would not loosen.

She was trapped in her own house and the monster was somewhere outside. Her son's body lay crumpled and lifeless just yards beyond her front steps. Somewhere in the bush lay her daughter-in-law's lifeless figure. And inside the house with her was the mangled body of her grandson, swaddled and tucked into his crib. Yewande collapsed into a chair and cried. It was all she knew to do. Not even the smell of burnt bean cakes and pork bothered her—they sizzled and popped and blackened in a pan of oil at least eleven inches deep.

Outside, somewhere close to her front door, the monster growled.

At first locking the old woman into the house alone had seemed a good idea. "Mama," Ekundayo had said to her, taking her own hands in his while he spoke, "that monster killed my *son*. It pushed through that door and stole him from his bed while he slept." The old woman thought of the toddler; he had been soft and helpless, barely able to walk. Had he smiled when he saw the animal towering over him, thinking it was one of his toys that had come to play with him? Did the beast growl; was the baby afraid? Did her grandson cry out when its teeth sliced through its flesh, or was death merciful and quick? She shuddered. She never heard the baby cry while she slept in her own bed. She only heard her daughter-in-law's screams when she found the empty crib and bloody sheets. The trail of blood led out of the house, and the door was wide open, swinging lazily back and forth in the late-night breeze.

"Mama, the monster killed my *wife*," her son had told her. Yewande remembered Ekundayo trying to calm his wife before grabbing a lantern and running out into the darkness. She was beyond consolation, and when the sun rose the next morning she walked out of the house, her grief worn on her body like a robe two sizes too small: tight and constricting. There were no neighbors for at least two days' travel, and no animal had ever been so bold as to break into a human's house, at least not in her lifetime. "It was evil spirits. It had to be," the old woman remembered thinking as she heard her daughter-in-law's wails coming from the other side of the trees. They were faint, but still her ancient ears heard them. She heard her scream as well; it was primal and defiant, and then she heard the roar. And then silence.

When darkness fell her son walked through the front door, his face twisted in grief. In his hands was something wet and lifeless—the body of his son. Or, rather, what was left of it. Yewande nearly fainted when she saw the mass of gristle and bone; it had been mauled and torn and eaten. Had it not been for the swaddles still wound about its feet she would have never known it was the body of her grandson, but she recognized her own cloth, fabric laboriously sewn by her own twisted fingers. "It can't be," she said.

"Where is my wife?" Ekundayo had asked.

"She went out there." Her voice was a whisper and she pointed at the door. "I couldn't stop her, and you weren't here to help me. She went out there. I heard her calling the baby's name. I heard her scream. I haven't seen her since."

Something lunged against the front door. The wood bulged in but it held. The old woman screamed, and Ekundayo jumped, the small body falling to the floor at his feet with a thud. Yewande felt sick to her stomach and held her mouth. Something outside growled; it was almost a maniacal scream, not quite an animal but definitely not human. "Evil spirits," she whispered, backing away from the door.

It growled again, clawing at the door. "Not evil spirits, mother. It's a leopard." Again and again it pummeled the door with the weight of its body as Ekundayo pushed a heavy chair across the floor, jamming it against the door; and just in time as it gave way, and a powerful claw sliced through the open space. He pushed the chair harder; the paw was caught in the door and the leopard screamed in pain. It pulled at its own foot; in a burst of fur, gristle, and gore, the leopard pulled its paw free.

Ekundayo listened as it ran out into the night.

The father sat in that chair against the door, staring at his son's mangled body; stiffly, the old woman walked to the baby's room and returned with a blanket. Carefully she bent to the floor and swaddled it. Tears stung her red eyes; she shuffled back to the child's room. Ekundayo heard her close the door, her feet dragging on the wood floor as she walked back to the main room. Exhausted, she sat in another chair across from her son; ancient mother and middle-aged son sat like that all night, too exhausted to move but too afraid to sleep.

When morning came it was almost a relief.

"I'm going to Ondo," he had said.

"What?" She was barely listening. Sleep was close, but fear kept it at arm's length.

"I'm going to Ondo," he said again.

The old woman sat up in her chair, her head shaking, and her mouth forming the word *no* even though fear stole her voice. "Something is not right with that leopard, mother. It is a monster. Leopards don't attack humans. They most certainly don't break into houses. It must be sick— I don't know . . . distemper? Rabies? Or maybe it's just lost its fear of humans. Maybe I can find a hunter in Ondo who will come back to hunt it and kill it. If it leaves the country and goes to the city before anyone knows, things will go badly. And if I don't do something, it will kill us as well."

"If you go out there, it will kill you." Yewande's voice was barely a whisper; fear was heavy, and it bore down on her chest. She could barely breathe.

"And if I stay here we will both die. Even if we bar the door and stay inside we will die. We will starve. I have to go."

"I will go with you." She stood; her body was stiff from a night spent sitting in the chair.

"No, mother," Ekundayo got up and put his hands around his mother's waist. He helped her to stand. "You can barely walk. You're too old to ride a horse. You're too sick to make the journey. We will never make it if you go. I must go alone."

"I'm afraid!" Her face twisted and tears came. "If you leave me that monster will come in here and I will die."

"It won't get in, mother. I promise you. The leopard is strong enough to force the door open, but it's not strong enough to break the wood or the frame. The latch is old but the wood is solid. I'll tether the door shut once I'm outside. I'll tether it well. It won't be able to get in."

"And I won't be able to get out!"

"When I come back with the hunter in a few days we'll get you out, after we kill the beast. You have enough food here to last you for days. You'll be fine." Her eyes pleaded with him, *Please do not go!* But his mind was made up. "Mother, the leopard killed my *son*. It pushed through that door and stole him from his bed while he slept." When still she did not answer he said, ""Mama, the leopard killed my *wife*." When still she did not answer, he took her head in his hands and made her look in his eyes. "Mother, if I do not go it will kill us both. This is our only chance."

"Go," she said. Yewande sat back in her chair, her hands clasped over her heart. "Go and find your hunter. Just be careful. And come back for me." That was when the tears came; they were hot and free. Her son ran through the house gathering what he needed. Yewande busied herself making a meal—while her son looked for what he needed, she put bean cakes and pork in a pan of oil, and set it over the household hearth to heat and fry. As the smell of food filled the house, Ekundayo found a rope and tied it to the door's handle so tight that no human hands could undo it; and then, he found a spike. It was long, and he tied the rope to the top of that. Giving his mother a light kiss on the cheek, he went outside and shut the door behind him, and Yewande could hear Ekundayo grunting as he hammered the spike deep in the earth. He gave the door a gentle shove, and when it didn't give, a more forceful one. It barely budged.

"But you must eat before you go," Yewande said. She was afraid to be left alone.

Through the small crack he called out to her, "I love you, and I'll be back with help soon."

"But you can't leave without eating," she pleaded.

"I'll be safe, mother. Stay inside."

"Stay inside," she thought. *"As if I have any choice now."* The pork-and-bean cakes were burning; she could smell them but she paid them no mind.

That was when the monster came: perhaps it had been in the bush watching from behind the trees, or perhaps it was just blind luck, a random attack. But as she stood beside the door peering through the crack she heard the monster growl; and she saw her son's face twist into a mask of fear. There was another growl, almost a roar; it was a sound not belonging to this world, the scream of a maniac. She heard her own son scream; and by instinct he ran to the house and tried to rip the door open and run back inside. When the door ripped itself from his hand and slammed shut in his face Yewande screamed; she clawed at the handle and tried to open it but it wouldn't budge. She heard fast, heavy footsteps down the front porch, another scream, and then silence.

Now she stood peering outside the door. Her son's mauled body lay only yards from the house; it was all blood and gore. And the leopard was nowhere to be seen.

"He'll kill me next," she said, shutting the door.

The smell of burnt food was strong; the oil sizzled and popped as thick smoke filled the house. Outside the leopard sniffed the air; the smell of burnt meat was tempting and he walked up to the front door. As the oil sizzled and the old woman listened to its pop, the leopard scratched at the door. The latch was broken from Ekundayo's futile attempt to get back inside, and it swung open as far as the rope would let it. The monster growled. Yewande screamed, and when the beast heard her scream it went silent. The old woman stared at its red eyes as it pushed its head through the crack; she shuddered at the foam that dripped from its mouth onto the floor. There was madness in the creature's eyes. And that's when fear left and anger came.

"Evil thing!" she seethed, backing away from the door. The room was silent except for the pan of oil sizzling over the fire. The head backed out and a great paw with razor sharp claws sliced the air between them. Then the leopard's head came back, and with its paw it pulled at the wood floor, trying to pull itself inside. The door held firm and the beast was stuck.

"You killed my grandson," the old woman hissed. Carefully she wound bands of cloth around her hands, and backed up to the fireplace.

The leopard growled.

"You killed my daughter-in-law, and my son."

The leopard hissed; without turning her back to it, she reached into the fire and lifted the pot of sizzling oil from the embers. Carefully she shuffled back to the front door, the pan shaking and hot oil spilling to the floor.

"And now you want to eat me." The old woman stood just inches from the beast's paws; they stared each other down, greasy foam still spilling from the leopard's mouth to the floor. She saw the claw marks on the carefully polished wood, wood she spent years wiping and mopping and scrubbing while her only son was still a child. Wood that was as ancient as the skin on her bones; wood that would still be there long after she was dead.

"So eat this," she hissed, flinging the pot of oil with all her might. The oil made a graceful arc in the air between her and the beast; everything seemed to move slowly, and the old woman watched as it reached out like a wave and caressed the leopard's head. The pork-and-bean cakes were blackened; they rolled to the floor, and the sick scent of burnt flesh filled the room just before the sick thud of cast iron cracking bone assaulted her ears.

The leopard screamed. It twisted and bit at the air, trying to free itself from the door, its one claw slashing its own flesh where the oil burnt its fur, blackened its skin, and melted its eyes. Yewande watched as the leopard lunged backwards and pulled itself free, writhing and twisting on the earth before it tripped over her son's lifeless body, falling still at his mauled feet.

She walked through the oil, slipping and almost falling before grabbing the door to catch herself. With her one good eye she peered out the crack; it was wider, and she saw the tether that was pounded in the earth was all but ready to give away from the leopard's strength. She gave it one more good pull; the line pulled free from the earth.

Yewande stood there and watched as the leopard took its last breath.

The Osogbos (Misfortunes) and the Àkùko (Rooster)

From the Odu Owani Meji (11-11)

Eshu can help us: Eshu can hurt us.

Àkùko had ashé; not a creature in the forest denied that.

All the animals from the smallest bird to the largest elephant sought him out for advice when their lives soured. He spent his days with these clients, prescribing spells and witchcraft to solve their problems. Sometimes he divined for them and although his ashé was not divination, he had studied enough to be competent in its practice. His work brought him wealth, and with that wealth he built a house that was spacious by any human's standards. The rooster lived well.

Ekún was jealous of Àkùko; he, too, had ashé, but instead of skills at magic or witchcraft or divination, his ashé lay in both his cunning as a predator and his dark alliances with the creatures known as the osogbos. Animals sought him out for his advice, but when he was unable to provide magic as a solution they were disappointed. When he suggested gifts to the osogbos as if they were ebós to the orishas, many refused and ran to the diviners. Ekún knew the osogbos well; they were his best friends and if given the right gifts as bribes would leave any animal alone—for a time. Ikú (Death), Ano (Illness), Aro (Terminal Illness), Eyo (Tragedy), Arayé (Misfortune), Inya (War), Ona (Affliction), Ofo

(Loss), Ogo (Sorcery), Akoba (Suffering), Fitibo (Sudden Death), Égba (Paralysis), Oran (Crimes), Epe (Curse), Ewon (Imprisonment), and Eshe (General Afflictions) were Ekún's best friends. It was because of these unnatural alliances that the animals were afraid of him; and when faced with an insurmountable obstacle, they chose to seek out Àkùko before they sought out Ekún. The wisest animals chose light over darkness, and it made Ekún angry.

Such was his anger that he stalked Àkùko. When he walked through the forest, Ekún was there, walking in shadows and watching. When he was inside his house sleeping, Ekún was outside peering through the windows. And when his own home was empty of clients, Ekún hid outside Àkùko's house, watching the rooster's clients come and go. Today was such a day—Ekún watched the rooster's house. It stood in a clearing in the middle of the forest surrounded by thick bush, and Ekún crouched low in the bushes as he spied; with jealousy his tail flicked and his eyes narrowed. A constant line of clients formed outside the rooster's front door, and one by one they waited their turn to see Àkùko. This day his stomach rumbled with hunger—it had been days since he had eaten, such was his poverty. "It's not fair," he said to himself, trembling. "My ashé is as good as the rooster's ashé, but everyone comes to him for help and not me." He backed out of the bush in which he hid slowly, and when he was sure he was out of earshot, he ran through the forest.

He went to the house of Ikú.

It was not hard to find Ikú; when she was idle during the daylight hours she sought out the darkest part of the forest. Even there, she sat in the darkest shadows. Ekún found her alone; she was always alone. The air around her was cold, chilled with the ashé of death; dark shadows wrapped themselves around her like a thick quilt. Her gaze made him shiver; it was ominous, filled with unfathomable secrets. She smiled at Ekún; and as always, he was conflicted by that smile. While her figure was uninviting and imposing, her smile belied inner warmth that made her seem loving. Reverently he crouched before her; it was an act of subservience, and he waited, with dread, for her cold hands to offer a blessing. He shivered at their touch.

"Why have you come?" Ikú asked. In spite of the coldness of her touch and the darkness of her gaze, her voice was musical and pleasant, loving in spite of her chilling form. It was both her smile and her voice that made him trust her in spite of her preternatural nature; for most, death was little more than the end of life, but Ekún found in her a willing friend, and he cherished that friendship not only for what she could do for him, but also because they were kindred souls. *"We are both hunters, you and I,"* she had once told him, and he had agreed it was true.

Ekún stood up on all fours, his tail wagging nervously. "You know I wouldn't come to you if it wasn't important."

Ikú knew. For most of his favors, he approached the osogbos who were less fatal. Rarely did Ikú lash out at an animal unless she meant to kill it, and once a creature was in her gaze, it was as good as dead. Her prey had little chance to escape. "I know. You rarely come to see me. You seem to fear me."

"You are imposing, my friend." Ikú smiled at him. "Except when you smile," he added. Ikú laughed, and her laughter lifted the shadows a bit; but when she grew silent the darkness seemed deeper.

"Ekún, you flatter me. You of all creatures know you have nothing to fear by seeking me out. It is only when I seek *you* out that you know your time has come. Only then should you be afraid."

That relaxed him. He sat back on his haunches. "Ikú, you know my work. When the osogbos threaten the animals of the forest, the animals come to me, and when I discover which osogbo plagues them, I offer to . . . intervene . . . for a price."

"Yes, I know. You have been a friend to us all since you and I first met."

Ekún bit his lip. "Why did you not kill me that day? When we ran into each other? You came to me."

"It was an accident, Ekún. You were young, and both of us were running through the forest without watching our way. I was not looking for you that day. Ours is a friendship born by chance."

"And may we always be friends," Ekún thought. He shuddered. "Now, I have a problem, Ikú, and I don't know where to turn. Àkùko is a miracle worker. He divines. He prescribes ebó. He knows magic and witchcraft that renders the osogbos powerless over the animals he helps, and no one comes to me anymore."

Ikú was silent as she thought about this.

"Worse, when he prescribes ebó to the orishas or gives magic to save his clients from the osogbos, they are rendered powerless over that creature, and they get nothing in return. I am starving because I have no work. And I can't imagine any of the osogbos are doing much better now that the animals of the forest no longer pay tribute to them. Àkùko needs to be dealt with."

Her voice lost its warmth, and it was as icy as the shadows when she said, "Àkùko needs to die. And then, he can't work any more miracles or force my brothers and sisters into submission."

"My thoughts exactly," said Ekún. At that moment he was never happier to have Ikú as a good friend.

It was early evening when Ikú and Ekún crept up on Àkùko's house; he was leaving, locking the door, and holding a package tightly to his chest. A horse was saddled and tied to a post outside; he untied it and jumped on. Ekún almost laughed when he saw the rooster straddling a horse, but then he became angry. "He can afford a horse but I cannot," he whispered.

"Quiet," whispered Ikú. "What is he holding?"

As Àkùko broke into a quick gallop, something primal stirred inside Ekún; he crouched and flicked his tail and then he sped after the horse. Ikú was behind him. "Wait," she called out, "what is he holding?"

Spooked, the horse broke into a breakneck gallop; behind them, Ekún ran as fast as he could. He was as fast as the horse, but the steed had a head start of quite a few yards. Ikú stretched out and spread as

quickly as the darkness, and when Àkùko realized he was being followed he threw the package behind him as he flew past the crossroads.
It was a mixture of epó and okra slime, and it spread like melted butter
over the road.

Ekún and Ikú slid and crashed into the trees. Àkùko kept galloping away into the distance. The forest rumbled and shook when Ikú
screamed in pain and anger. "I'll get him if it's the last thing I do!" she
swore to Ekún.

Àkùko kept galloping, pushing his horse as fast as it would go. He
rode all the way to Orúnmila's house.

The wise diviner knew why he came. Just that morning he was divining for himself, and the oracle told him that a client was coming with
all the osogbos in the world on his heels. When Àkùko jumped off his
horse so quickly that he crashed into Orúnmila's house, he was not surprised—just annoyed at the rooster's carelessness. He threw open his
door; and smiled when he saw his next client . . . was the rooster.

"Inside, quickly," he said. The rooster wasted no time, and Orúnmila
locked the door behind him. "So the forest's own miracle worker has
come to see me?"

He was breathless when he said, "I divined for myself, and I made
the ebó, but I barely escaped with my own life. Ekún and his friend Ikú
are after me."

"It's worse than that, I'm afraid. You escaped, but you didn't solve
your problems. Ekún, Ikú, and now all the osogbos are after you. You
only angered Ikú, and she gathers reinforcements outside these walls."

"But why?"

Orúnmila took a deep breath. "Your skills at divination are lacking,
I'm afraid. You rely on magic—witchcraft and charms. Instead of work-
ing with the orishas and appeasing them so they can help you and your
clients, you work magic constantly to strip the osogbos of power yourself.
You might be a powerful sorcerer in your own way, but you are not a god.
You use your magic to fight, and he who fights will know what war is."

"So I am as good as dead? Nothing can save me?"

"Ebó can save anyone," said Orúnmila. "Today, we will make ebó to Eshu. And he will be the one who will save you."

Together, Àkùko and Orúnmila lined a wicker basket with red and black cloth; together, they filled it with toasted corn, cigars, and eleven bottles of rum. Quietly, Orúnmila opened his front door and Àkùko pushed the ebó outside so Eshu could find it. When the osogbos saw the rooster pushing the basket outside, they rose up; like a great, dark cloud they came rushing at the front door. As quickly as he opened it, Orúnmila pulled the frightened rooster back inside and slammed it shut; he locked it, and listened as the osogbos pounded it, trying to break it. But Orúnmila's door was well protected by both ebós and charms, and no matter how hard they tried they were unable to break it.

Shadows fell over the windows as they encircled the house once more. "The windows!" screamed Àkùko, his voice high and shrill like a woman's. "They will break in through the windows!"

"They won't," said Orúnmila, rubbing the rooster's head to soothe him. "The osogbos are dreadfully stupid creatures. They only try to come in by the front door, the door closest to the street. They are easily kept outside. Likewise, we are locked inside if we hope to stay safe."

Quietly they waited, listening to the osogbos' fearful howls and the hungry growls of Ekún. Everything went quiet when there were three knocks at the door; and the shadows receded. Orúnmila peeked out. It was Eshu, and he was eating corn and drinking rum, all the while smiling a crooked smile. "I've heard that you need my help?"

Orúnmila let the orisha inside. The howls and growls began again from the forest.

All night Eshu ate; he ate in silence and looked at the rooster with a smile on his face. Orúnmila fell asleep in his chair while Eshu ate, but the rooster was unnerved. *"He looks at me as if I am food,"* he thought to himself.

All night long, as if the growls of Ekún were not enough the preternatural cries of the osogbos wailed through the darkness. *"I won't survive this night,"* Àkùko thought to himself.

Dawn came, and Eshu finished eating. "See? You survived this night after all!"

The rooster trembled. Eshu could read his thoughts.

Orúnmila woke up and stretched; when he saw that Eshu finished his corn and rum he asked, "Are you still hungry?"

"No, I'm quite full," he said. "Now, about the rooster's problem . . ."

"What can we do?" asked Orúnmila.

"Yes, what can I do?" asked Àkùko.

"It's no longer just your problem," said Eshu. "You brought osogbo to Orúnmila's house. They won't leave until they get what they want, or unless we trick them first."

"How do we do that?" asked Orúnmila. "I can't live with evil right outside my front door."

"It's simple, Orúnmila. I'll carry the rooster away in this basket, covered by this cloth. And then once I leave with the rooster, you can let them come in and try to have the rooster."

"Excuse me?" asked Àkùko. Eshu's words confused him—he was going to whisk him away to safety *and* let the osogbos have him? "Exactly how does that work again?"

"It's not your business," said Eshu. "Just get in the basket." Without faith but having no other options, Àkùko did as he was told. He climbed inside the basket. Eshu covered him with red and black cloth, and then divided himself in two.

"How?" Orúnmila asked.

"Don't ask," said Eshu. "You wouldn't understand." He picked up one of the two baskets sitting at his feet, the one covered with red and black cloth. The basket filled with corn and rum remained on the floor.

"But . . ." said Orúnmila.

"Is there a problem?" asked Eshu.

The rooster stood on the floor beside the basket; he was trembling.

"How did he get out of the basket?" asked Orúnmila.

"I told you no questions." Eshu threw open the door and left with the basket slung over his shoulder. Inside, the rooster sat very still; he was afraid, but dared not tremble or squawk. Ekún, Ikú, and the osogbos stood aside while Eshu walked slowly into the forest, and when they saw the door to Orúnmila's house still open, they stormed inside.

"Get out of my house!" ordered Orúnmila. He stood strong, but was afraid.

Eshu sat in Orúnmila's chair, drinking rum and eating corn. The rooster trembled and hid behind his feet.

"We want him," said Ikú, pointing at the rooster. "He has caused quite enough trouble for us." So afraid was Àkùko that he scattered droppings on the floor behind him. Had Orúnmila not been afraid of the osogbos, he would have been angry at Àkùko for that.

"Well you can't have him," said Eshu. "He is mine. I'm eating my corn and drinking my liquor, and when I am done I will eat him."

"I marked him for death yesterday, Eshu. You have no right to interfere."

"If you think you're strong enough, Ikú, you can try to take him from me. But I warn you it won't go well." Eshu picked up the rooster and ripped off his head; where he sat, he drank his blood not spilling a drop. Orúnmila's eyes all but popped out of his head in surprise, and Ikú howled.

When the rooster was quite dead and lay lifeless at Eshu's feet, she recovered her composure. "It all ends the same. Our work is done. Let's leave."

"Wait!" roared the leopard. "He caused trouble for me, too. I want to feast on his flesh."

Eshu was about to turn over the rooster's carcass when Orúnmila intervened. "I provided that sacrifice. By our laws and customs, that meat goes to me. Try to take it . . . if you think you're able." Ekún growled once, all his hairs standing on end; and then he stood down.

"Never come here again," warned Eshu. "And never think to look for this Àkùko again. Ebó was made here today, powerful magic and sacrifice, which none of you will ever hope to understand. If I ever catch any of you overstepping your bounds on this again, it will not end well. It won't end well for any of you." Eshu eyed the leopard hungrily. "I do so love leopard flesh. And your fur is so warm on a cold, dark night."

Ekún fled Orúnmila's house that day followed by all the osogbos. When they were scattered back into the world, the diviner turned to Eshu and asked, "How could you kill him after he made ebó? How could you do it?"

"That wasn't him," said Eshu, "and this isn't me. If I'm nothing else, I'm tricky and full of surprises. And you, Orúnmila, owe the real me a real rooster. I saved you today just as I saved the Àkùko."

Orúnmila was about to thank Eshu when he realized—he was talking only to himself.

The Earth and the Wind
From the Odu Owani Meji (11-11)

One never knows what destiny will
bring—only ebó can save us.

Owani divined for Afefe (the wind) and Ayé (the ground) on the day that the two decided to travel together into the world. "If you want to be successful on the earth," she told them, "you both need to make sacrifice with your own hands. You need to make ebó to both Eshu and your own guardian angels. Offer a palm leaf, a red parrot feather, and feed your orishas with all the animals they eat. Cook the ashés and season their meats well. Do all these things, and you will be prosperous in the material world."

Ayé was stable and strong, full of good character and patience, and he took his time making his ebós. To both Obatalá and Eshu he made sacrifice with birds and goats, and he ended it all with the gift of a single

guinea hen. During the day he labored, plucking and skinning the animals and removing their inner organs. These he cooked with the blood
and fresh herbs from his garden. When he was done Ayé presented two
gourds—one to Obatalá and one to Eshu—each filled with their ashés.
He spent the rest of his day seasoning and cooking the meat. Lifting
the ashés from their shrines the next morning, he gave them platters
of freshly cooked meats, laying each plate on top of a single palm leaf
and placing a single red parrot feather beside each. Only when that was
done did he make preparations to go into the world.

While Ayé made sacrifice Afefe was impatient; she ran about heaven
listlessly, bored out of her mind yet too lazy to make ebó. "I will do it
later," she thought to herself. "Right now, I can barely think about the
trip at hand." She waited and waited for Ayé to finish his ebó, and when
he was done, hand in hand they left heaven together; quickly, they made
their way down to the material world.

At the gate between life and death, Olófin's ashé separated them,
and they were forced to walk separate paths.

Ayé landed on the earth with a thud, and quickly his form changed.
His spirit spread out over the world; he was thin and tenuous with no
more substance than a ghost, but after he spread he became solid, turning into the dirt on which all living things walked. So well had he made
sacrifice that Ayé became the foundation of all living creatures, both
the anchor and the foundation for everything else that came down
from heaven. He nourished the plants that nourished the animals, both
becoming the nourishment for humans created by Obatalá's hands.
Everything drew substance and strength from the rich, fertile earth;
and Ayé became a thing worshipped and loved, much as mortal beings
worship and love the orishas themselves.

For making ebó Ayé was blessed.

Afefe's feet never touched the earth; but quickly her form did
change. Her spirit spread out over the world; she was thin and tenuous
with no more substance than a ghost, but while Ayé became solid she
remained wispy and weak. "I don't like this!" she screamed, and in vain

she tried to rise back to heaven; but, the gates between the worlds were closed to her, and her yearning to return created the wind. Listlessly she floated through the sky; she rustled the leaves in the trees, and she caressed the earth with phantom arms. Nothing paid her any mind.

For not making ebó, Afefe was cursed—forced to wander the world without substance or form.

That is why we draw our sustenance from the earth and not the wind; that is why we walk on Ayé and not Afefe. That is why we adore the earth and pay little mind to the breezes that blow across her face. And that is why we make ebó in Owani Meji—so that we are strong and enduring like the earth, and not weak and ephemeral like the wind.

12
PATAKÍS FROM THE COMPOSITES OF EJILA SHEBORA

The Lands of Lesa and Mogue
From the Odu Ejila Oché (12-5)

Bitterness cannot turn sweet, but
sweet things can go bad.

The town of Mogue was filled with the rich scent of damp earth, and when the breeze stirred amid the streets there came through the village the heavy odor of the blood, or the more acrid scent of the decayed bodies. In Lesa it was no different, but the stench was worse and people traveled the streets with scarves wound about their mouths and noses.

For the field between the two towns was strewn with bodies and blood; the earth was caked with it, the soil blackened, saturated and unable to suck it down as it was spilled. Like red jelly it lay on the ground. This was the field where the warriors of Lesa and Mogue fought—it lay stretched between their towns, a nether land that neither owned but both wanted for themselves. For decades one village had tried to claim the land; its people would spread out over the rolling hills and begin to build, and when they were done, in the night and under the cover of darkness, the warriors from the other town would march with torches and burn it all to the ground. Children—silenced; women—raped; men—murdered; and the war had gone on for decades. No one remembered how it began. No one cared.

The earth was angry, hot as it was with all the blood. The yams and corn planted seasons ago by one of the villages still grew, and the spirit of the earth sent a rot that covered them like black silk. When the wind blew, it carried their spores across the fields and into the towns. Soon each village was covered in black dust and they swore, "Those people in the other village are sorcerers. They send this to us." When the weakest of each town, the elderly and the children, developed fevers and sores they drew arms. Again, as they had for decades, both towns prepared for war.

Yet war would not be.

For the earth, indeed, was angry, and by the time the armies were ready to battle they, too, fell ill. Soon neither town had anyone left to fight, and the villagers languished and died among the black rot. Both became ghost towns filled with bodies; and once everyone was dead the earth, again, knew peace.

Remember this: the earth has teeth and it will eat you, and no one will escape her wrath.

The Hunter and the Leopard
From the Odu Ejila Unle (12-8)

The leopard, after spending a few nights with hunger, is still stronger than a well-fed man.

The hunter was a gentle man; he was skilled at the hunt but only went when his family was in need of food. One morning when their store of food was low he had no choice but to track prey. In the heart of the forest he found a huge stone, and as he walked around the stone he discovered a small opening into the earth. He kneeled down beside the great rock and tried to peer inside.

He saw a leopard.

"Kind hunter," said the leopard, crouching down to look pitiful, "do not be afraid of me. I am gentle. Many days ago I fell into this trap. After the earth gave way a huge stone rolled down over me and I have been here for days. I will die if I do not get out soon. Please help me."

"If I help you," said the hunter, "once you are free you will eat me. It is the way of your kind. I would be foolish to set you free." And with those words the hunter stood up and started to walk away. He thought for a moment about killing the leopard where he stood, but decided against it. There was no sport in such a kill, and it would not be fair to the animal.

"Wait," screamed the leopard, shaking with fear. "Do not leave me. I swear that I will not eat you if you let me out of this hole."

The hunter turned to face the rock and the hole, and for quite some time thought about setting the leopard free. And then, he set him free. Once the leopard was free he stood looking at the hunter, drooling.

"You are not a kind leopard after all, are you?" he said. "You stand there thinking about eating me even though I saved you, and even though you promised you would not. You wish to repay the good I did you with evil."

The leopard hung his head. "I am sorry. It is just that I am so hungry. I cannot help myself."

The hunter stood there with his crossbow raised, pointed at the leopard's heart; he thought about killing him, but lowered his crossbow instead. "I will make a pact with you, leopard. We will seek out three animals and tell them what I have done. We will ask them if it is right that a good be repaid with evil. And if they say it is right, we will fight to the death."

They traveled separately down the same road, the leopard trailing far behind the hunter. In time the hunter spied an ox. The hunter asked him, "Ox, is it true that good is often repaid with evil?"

The ox said, "It is true that good is repaid with evil. When I was young, I plowed the earth without complaint and now that I am old, they take me to the butcher block."

"That's one animal who agrees," said the leopard. "Two more and I will eat you."

"Two more, and I will try to kill you," said the hunter.

The hunter and the leopard continued to walk through the forest. "Let us hurry. I am very hungry," said the leopard.

"And my family is hungry as well," said the hunter.

They came to a horse and the hunter asked, "Horse, is it true that good is repaid with evil?"

The horse said, "Good is repaid with evil. It happens every day. When I was young I was pampered by my owner, and now that I am old I have to find my own food in the fields."

The leopard said to the hunter, "It is time for me to eat you."

The hunter answered, "We made a pact, and we still have one more animal to ask."

They walked for hours until they spied a fox. The hunter called out to him, "Good with good, is that what you would repay?"

And the fox said, "That a good is repaid with good?" He was quiet and stared warily at the two. "What kind of a question is this? Explain yourself, hunter, because I trust neither you nor the leopard and I want to run."

The leopard sat back on his haunches and tried to look innocent. "I was walking through the forest and I fell in a hole. The hole was a trap, and after I fell a great rock rolled over on top of me. I sat there, in darkness, for many days. I was unable to free myself."

The fox said, "This is a lie. I do not believe you."

The leopard answered, "How are you going to tell me that this is a lie?"

The fox said, "Because your kind lie all the time. Show me how it happened and then I might believe you."

The leopard led the hunter and the fox back through the forest; the fox, not trusting either, walked behind them ready to run at the first sign of trouble. When the three got to the trap the leopard said, "This is how it happened." He jumped in the hole and told the hunter, "Roll the rock back over the top." The hunter obliged. The fox sat back and smiled. "See?" he called from deep in the pit, "This is how it happened. Now, hunter, show him how you let me out."

The fox said, "Kind hunter, leave him here . . . for he would have never repaid your kindness with kindness. He is a leopard, and the minute your back was turned and your weapon lowered, he would have eaten you where you stood."

The fox and hunter walked away from the pit and left the leopard trapped beneath the earth.

The Tale of the Spiders
From the Odu Ejila Meji (12-12)

The spider said to her children, "Just when you are beginning to know life I will know death."

Ilere* lay in her bed wrapped in cool, white sheets. Her only light was the dying flame of a candle that sputtered and danced against the darkness. As it flickered she could see the soft shadow of a spider's web spun high in the corner of her room; in its center a spider worked, reinforcing an already tight ball of silk. Her legs and mouth moved tirelessly

---

*Ilere is a "secret" name for the odu Ejila Shebora.

and the ball grew. With weary eyes Ilere watched. Her eyes grew heavy and closed as she slipped in the place where the worlds of sleep and reality folded on themselves, and still, with closed eyes, it seemed that she could see the spider working.

When her spinning was done the spider lay beside the ball and sighed. "Just when you are beginning to know life I will die," she whispered to her unborn.

Ilere sat up pulling her sheets to her chest. "Who said that?" she called out.

On a silk thread as thin as the finest hair, the spider let herself down to Ilere's pillow. They were unmoving, staring: Ilere at the spider and the spider at Ilere. Finally the spider spoke, "Just when my children are beginning to know life I will die. It is the nature of our kind."

The young woman let her sheets fall. In dreams it was not unusual for animals to speak. *"Is this a dream?"* she asked herself. *"Spiders cannot speak. It must be a dream."* Then she said to the spider, "It was like that with me. I am Ilere, daughter of Olokban and Tolokban.* They died when I was quite young. I never really knew them."

The spider spoke, "My children will never know me at all." Spinning her egg sack left her weary, and gently she laid her own head on the pillow. "They will never know me. They will never know my stories. I don't even know the stories of my ancestors. There was no one to tell them to me when I was a child."

"The spider did speak," Ilere thought. *"This must be a dream."* She pushed her hair back from her face and spoke, "That must be sad to not know the stories of your kind. Where are your elders? Do they not teach?"

"No, there are no elders to teach. We are our own elders." The spider sighed again; it was gentle and drawn out, like a soft summer breeze in the forest. "We all live in one big cycle. Together we are born. Together we mate. Together we lay our eggs, and together we die just as

---

*Olokban and Tolokban are the names of Ejila Shebora's earthly, mortal parents.

our young hatch. We never see our fathers or our mothers. We never see our children. We have no connection with our past. We are cut off and alone, each generation being the sum of our kind."

"I know your stories," said Ilere. "I grew up with them when I was a child."

"I wish I knew our stories," said the spider. "I wish there were someone to tell my children our stories."

Ilere smiled; gently, she moved the pillow on which the spider lay closer to her. "I will tell your stories," she said, "and the world will remember them." Her voice was soft as she spoke to the spider.

The first of your kind were not born on earth; they were born in heaven, creatures of spirit, not flesh. They were soft and weak, but they were happy living where there was neither sickness nor death. Still the more curious of your kind watched as all the animals began the journey to earth; and when humans were created they marveled at the creatures who walked with two legs and mastered their environments with two hands. When the insects rose from the earth and walked fearlessly among giants, the spiders were jealous. They, too, wanted to know the new world Olódumare created. In mass they went to the diviners to find out what they had to do to live on the earth.

They told the spiders that the world was a dangerous place for creatures as small as they; but the spiders had seen the tiny insects flourishing without fear. They told the spiders that it was their right to settle in the material world, but as with all new ventures they were to make ebó; and they were warned to stay out of the cities—the forests were where they would live best. They were told that their numbers would be legion on the earth, that each female would renew their race yearly with thousands of progeny. Of all the creatures big and small few would be as blessed as they. The spiders liked the diviners' words and they agreed to everything. Quickly they made preparations to leave.

"The diviners have said that we will be legion on earth—our females will renew our race yearly. We do not need to make ebó," said the men.

"Let us prepare to leave now so we can make our way in the world. There is no time to waste!" The women were fearful, but they followed their men, and no one bothered to make ebó.

It was an unfortunate thing.

At first they were happy in the forests. Food was abundant, and although they were small their appetites were huge. When your ancestors came they feasted on the wild fruits and berries that grew freely among the bushes and trees. As they spread throughout the woods eventually they arrived at the edge of the wild lands—and before them stretched human civilization. Strange sights and smells seduced them; quickly they forgot the diviners' warnings and left the safety of the trees for the uncertainty of the cities.

The spider smiled as she listened to Ilere. "I have never lived in the woods," she said. "I have always been a house spider. Nor have I tasted fruits or berries. I live off the juices and blood of insects unlucky enough to be stuck in my web. It is a beautiful story, but I find no truth in it."

Ilere creased her brow. "I can tell you've never been told a story," she said. "Stories acquire strange twists and turns, and the way they begin is never the way they end. Be still little one, and let me tell you what happened."

It was dark when the spiders left the safety of the trees for the uncertainty of the civilized world; thousands of them walked the streets at night and found their way into houses and shops through the little cracks under the doors or in window frames. Some stayed outside making homes in the awnings while others took up residence in horse stables and gardens.

When the sun rose the next morning great cries went up in the city. Humans saw the big, hairy spiders in their homes and they were afraid. One by one screaming children and frantic woman stomped them with their feet or beat them with sticks. Soft and weak, the spiders succumbed. Hundreds were killed each day.

Elegguá was walking through town that day and he found one of the spiders cowering in the street under some trash. It was too afraid to move.

"Why are you trembling?" Elegguá asked the spider.

"The humans are trying to kill us," it said.

"Why did you come to the city? Did the diviners not warn you to stay in the forest?"

"We wanted to live among humans and learn of the wonders they created."

"Surely you can fight back," said Elegguá. "Did you not make ebó before you came to be strong?"

"We never made ebó. We were too anxious to come to the new world."

The spider trembled so violently with fear that the trash under which he hid rustled as if dancing in a breeze.

Gently, Elegguá picked up the spider. "You need to make ebó. Each of your kind was told to bring two iron needles and bunches of bitter herbs from the forest before you came into the world. These were so you could defend yourselves. And you were to feed me a goat, a rooster, and a guinea hen in exchange for my help. Do these things and I will help your kind survive in this world."

He sat the spider down on the dusty road; it ran as fast as it could to gather up the rest of the spiders. By nightfall they stood at the edge of the forest, each spider with two needles, bitter herbs, and together they got the animals Elegguá required. When all was ready the orisha came to accept his ebó.

Dreamily the spider smiled; she was weary, and she wore sleep on her head like a gauzy scarf, loosely wrapped. "I cannot see any of us having the strength to gather needles or herbs or animals. Are you sure this is how it happened?" she asked.

"Your bodies might be soft and squishy but the first of your kind had great strength, I am sure," said Ilere. "If not, how did they gather the ebó, indeed?"

After Elegguá ate his goat, his rooster, and his guinea, he lifted the iron needles from the spider closest and said, "Open your mouth. Wide." The spider did as he was told. Gently Elegguá pushed the needles into his gums and said, "Bite down."

The needles held fast—the small creature had razor sharp teeth. One by one Elegguá put the needles in the mouths of all the spiders; each had teeth that were razor sharp and iron-strong.

"But these are too small to defend ourselves against the humans," said the spiders. "They are large. Our mouths are small and our teeth tiny. To bite them would be no more than an annoyance, and they would crush us as we bit."

"Use your teeth to suck the sap from the bitter plants," Elegguá ordered. "It will taste horrible, but suck on each leaf until it is a dry shell."

Great moans rose from the mass of spiders as they sucked the leaves and branches dry. The herbs were bitter, bitter to the point that their lips puckered and their mouths froze in a useless grimace. When they were done they tried to open their mouths; but they were unmoving, frozen into tiny slits so small they all but lost the power of speech.

"Our mouths are useless!" screamed the spiders. Their words were almost unrecognizable, but Elegguá understood their speech. One spider ran to a nearby bush and tried to open his mouth wide enough to eat a berry. It was useless. "We will starve! We cannot eat!"

There was panic at the forest's edge, and Elegguá's voice rose to drown them all out. "You've made ebó and your nature has changed. You will not starve. You will just eat another way!" A cricket wandered into their midst; he was unafraid of the spiders even though their numbers that day were legion. They were too soft to hurt him, or so he thought.

"Quickly," said Elegguá, "one of you try to bite that cricket."

The spiders were loath to hurt another creature, but so upset was one spider at the changes made that he attacked the cricket out of anger. His two tiny, razor sharp teeth sank into its soft flesh. A drop of thick poison dripped down his fangs and into the cricket's body.

It fell down, dead.

"Now you will see what good your mouths are. Bite him again, and this time suck."

The spider did as he was told; thick juices flooded his mouth. They were sweet, like fruit, and thick, like honey; they filled his belly with something that felt like gentle heat, and in a few moments a dry carcass hung from his teeth. He spit it out, and watched it lay crumpled on the ground.

"Your teeth are sharp and your mouths drip poison," said Eleggúa. "Just as a drop killed the cricket before his heart could beat a second time, so will a few drops cause pain and sometimes death to the humans. Once they learn your bites are poisoned they will think twice about trying to kill you. In time, they will run from you. You might be small, but now you are deadly."

That night the spiders marched back into town, and the next day when the humans sought to kill them the spiders fought back. Those who were bit suffered pain and torment, and when a few died from the bites they learned it was best to leave the spiders alone. The weak made ebó; and the weak became strong.

"Such a lovely story," said the spider. She lay on the pillow exhausted, barely moving. The chill of death was in her thin legs; it was heavy, and she found herself unable to move them. "I think my children will be hatching soon," she said.

"Why do you think that?" asked Ilere.

"Because I cannot move my legs. They are cold and they are heavy. And I am so tired. This must be what dying feels like. It's too bad there is no one to tell me. There is no one to sit with me and help me through it."

"I'm here," said Ilere. "If your time is close I won't leave you."

The spider smiled. "Why do we die just as our children are born? Did you grow up with a story for that, too?"

"I did," she said. "There is a reason you grow old, and then weak after you lay your eggs. Again, it has to do with the first of your kind."

The first generation of spiders enjoyed life on earth; they were strong and they were powerful predators. They spent their days hunting and their evenings eating their kills; and at night, they rested safely in the trees under a sky filled with stars. One morning when they awoke, they saw one of their own lying still, unmoving, and when they looked closer they saw the body had no breath. By nightfall the body was hard and fragile, and a light breeze knocked it from its branch. It fell to the earth and turned to dust.

"She is dead!" said one of the spiders. Never had they known death. In heaven they were immortal, but on earth their lives were ephemeral. Night after night it was the same—someone would die, sometimes dozens, and they saw their numbers dwindle.

The spiders sought out the orisha Elegguá.

"It is the nature of mortal beings to die," said Elegguá. "And in their place, their children grow. Where are your children?"

"We have none," said one of the spiders, fear in her voice. The chill of death touched her; she felt weak, and shivered.

"You have no children? All mortal creatures have children. That is why they make ebó in heaven before coming to earth—to make sure they are fruitful and multiply."

"We did not," said the spider weakly. "We never made ebó in heaven."

"And that is why you die with no children," said Elegguá. He looked at the female spiders one by one. "Ladies, follow me," he said. The males had puzzled faces as the females followed Elegguá through the forest, but they were too tired to protest and follow. Their bodies felt the chill of death, and they were weak.

Deep in the forest and well beyond the hearing of the males, Elegguá stopped. The female spiders stopped as well. "It is not your fault that you do not bear young," said Elegguá, "for it was the men of your race who told you that there was no need to make ebó. I will teach you how to mate. Unfortunately, when you are done you will be too weak to lay your eggs and spin the silk that will keep them safe . . . unless . . . you do one simple thing . . ." His voice trailed off; he was silent.

One of the females could stand the silence no longer. "What must we do?" she asked.

"You must eat your mate," Elegguá said. His voice was flat and a great cry rose among the females. "You are all dying," he said. "Even now, death nips at you. In a few days you will all be dead. None of you will live to see your children born. None of you will have the strength to bear children unless you draw on the strength of their fathers. All of this is because none of you had the foresight to make ebó. There is no other way."

Elegguá taught them how to seduce their males; he taught them how to join and copulate. Together the woman went back to their men; and in a great swarm, they seduced them. When they were done, they ate their mates.

None of them saw it coming—not a single male fought back.

One by one the female spiders scattered sadly thought the forest; they were like an aged tribe of amazons with no males left in their ranks. Soon their bodies swelled with eggs, and these they laid and wrapped in tough silk. Exhausted, they lay down to die and their bodies turned to dust while millions of small spiders awoke and marched through the forest.

Ilere looked down at the spider; she was sleeping, her tiny chest rising and falling slowly. She, too, was tired; she laid her head on the pillow and fell asleep watching the spider's breath slowing. As the light went out in her own head, she thought, *"A dream. This is all a dream . . . spiders don't talk, not really . . ."*

When she awoke the spider was dead. Her body was still and dry. She looked up to the corner where the thin web hung and watched as small dots scurried out of the silk sack. One by one they emerged, hanging on the thread as their brothers and sisters wriggled out.

On a line so thin it was almost invisible, one of the dots let herself down on Ilere's bed. In a voice so tiny it was barely a whisper, the spider asked, "Are you my mother?"

"So it was not a dream," Ilere thought. She shuddered. "No, I am not

your mother. She is dead." She looked where the old spider lay lifeless; her body was dried and drawn into itself, barely recognizable.

"What is 'dead'?" asked the little dot.

"It means she is no more. Her life ended just as you were born."

Hundreds of small dots descended silky webs to Ilere's bed. Thousands of eyes looked at her. "Would you like to know the story of your people? So you can be prepared for what lies ahead?"

Hundreds of voices said, "Yes." Ilere wrapped her sheets around herself and told them their stories.

GLOSSARY

Lucumí, and the original Yoruba from which it evolved, is a tonal language, like Chinese. Because the Afro-Cubans had neither the time nor the opportunity for formal education during slavery, many of these words have no consistent spelling. While I have tried to keep my own spellings consistent throughout my work, my spellings will differ from those of other authors in the field. However, the pronunciation of the words will be the same. For any Lucumí or Spanish term that does not have an accent mark, the proper emphasis goes on the second-to-last syllable in the word. To facilitate proper pronunciation, I have included the appropriate accent for all words that vary from this pattern. Vowel sounds for all non-English words will approximate those of the Spanish language.

Keep in mind the following points when pronouncing words:

- The *ch* sound is used in Lucumí and Spanish words; these languages have no *sh* sound.
- The *ñ* character (enye sound) is used in Spanish words only, and not Lucumí words.
- The *y* sound in Spanish has a slight edge to it, so that it sounds more like the English and Yoruba *j*. I have used *j* here whenever possible.

Also, note that in each glossary entry one or more words may be italicized. The italicization of a word indicates that it can be found in the glossary as well.

adele: Cowries left to the side unused during a reading with the *diloggún*.

afefe: Wind.

Ajé: This *orisha* controls luxury and wealth. Her normal guise is that of a beautiful woman.

akoba: A type of *osogbo* in which one's life in general is not good. When capitalized it denotes the spiritual principle of the same name.

àkùko: The *Lucumí* word for "rooster."

amalá: A staple food of the *orisha* Shangó; it is made of cornmeal.

ano: A *Lucumí* word that means "illness" or "disease." When capitalized it denotes the spiritual principle of the same name.

ará ikuo: The spirit of the skeleton. It was created by the *odu Unle*.

ará onú: A *Lucumí* word for those spirits (human) that inhabit heaven; also the name of the main character in the *patakís* from the *odu Ofún Ogundá* titled "How the Pigeon Was First Sacrificed."

arayé: Envy, ill will, arguments, evil tongues, and witchcraft. When capitalized it denotes the spiritual principle of the same name.

aro: A *Lucumí* word that means "durative illness" or "durative disease." When capitalized it denotes the spiritual principle of the same name.

ashé: A very dynamic universal force; the spiritual power of the universe. It has many meanings, among which are "grace," "life," "fate," "power," "talent," and "wisdom"; the meaning intended depends on its usage in speech. Most agree that life is ashé, and ashé is life.

ayé: Earth.

batá: A drumming festival held in honor of the *orishas*; also, the drums used at that festival.

composite odu: A pairing of *odu*. Each of the sixteen parent *odu* in the diloggún has sixteen-composite *odu;* there are 256 *composite odu* in total.

diloggún: The system of cowrie divination by which a priest or priest-ess of *Santería* learns the will of the *orishas;* also, the eighteen or twenty-one cowries shells that contain the soul of an orisha; also, the set of sixteen shells a priest casts to perform a divination. The exact meaning of the words depends on the context in which it is used.

ebó: An offering made to an *orisha*.

efun: A loosely packed, powdered chalk made from crushed eggshells.

égba: A *Lucumí* term that means "paralysis."

ejé oruko bale: The spirit of the blood; it was born in the *odu Osá Meji*.

Eji Oko: One of the sixteen *parent odu* in the *diloggún;* it consists of two mouths open on the mat.

Ejila Meji: One of the sixteen *composite odu* found in the family of *Ejila Shebora;* it opens when a casting of twelve mouths (*Ejila Shebora*) repeats itself.

Ejila Oché: One of the sixteen *composite odu* found in the family of *Ejila Shebora;* it opens when a casting of twelve mouths (*Ejila Shebora*) is followed by a casting of five mouths (*Oché*).

Ejila Osá: One of the sixteen *composite odu* found in the family of *Ejila Shebora;* it opens when a casting of twelve mouths (*Ejila Shebora*) is followed by a casting of nine mouths (*Osá*).

Ejila Shebora: One of the sixteen *parent odu* in the *diloggún;* it consists of twelve mouths open on the mat.

Ejila Unle: One of the sixteen *composite odu* found in the family of *Ejila Shebora;* it opens when a casting of twelve mouths (*Ejila Shebora*) is followed by a casting of eight mouths (*Unle*).

Ejioko Meji: One of the sixteen *composite odu* found in the family of

Eji Okó; this *odu* opens when a casting of two mouths (*Eji Okó*) is followed by another casting of two mouths.

Ejioko Owani: One of the sixteen *composite odu* found in the family of *Eji Okó;* this *odu* opens when a casting of two mouths (*Eji Oko*) is followed by a casting of eleven mouths (*Owani*).

ekún: A *Lucumí* word for "leopard."

elefanta: The Spanish word for a female elephant.

elefante: The Spanish word for "elephant."

Elegguá: An *orisha* also referred to as *Eshu*. He is often portrayed as fate, a young child, and an old man. Elegguá is the messenger of all the *orishas* and the first and last to be honored in every ceremony performed.

epe: Curse.

eshe: General afflictions.

Eshu: See *Elegguá*.

ewon: Imprisonment.

eyo: Tragedies.

fitibo: Sudden death.

gallina: Spanish, a hen.

gallo: Spanish, a rooster.

Ikú: Physical death or the personification of Death.

Ilere: A secret name of the odu *Ejila Shebora*.

inya: War.

ipari: The spirit controlling the limbs. It was born in the *odu Ogundá*.

ipejeun: The spirit governing the internal organs. It was born in the *odu Ogundá*.

Iroko: In Nigeria, Iroko refers to a specific tree that is sacred to the *orishas* and *Olódumare*. Iroko is also a powerful *orisha*. In the New World, the silk cotton tree is his sacred shrine.

Irosun: One of the sixteen *parent odu* in the *diloggún*; it is opened when four mouths fall face-up on the mat.

Irosun Meji: One of the sixteen *composite odu* found in the family of *Irosun*. It forms when a cast of four mouths (*Irosun*) repeats itself.

Irosun Odí: One of the sixteen *composite odu* found in the family of *Irosun*. It forms when a casting of four mouths (*Irosun*) is followed by a casting of seven mouths (*Odí*).

Irunmole: The first *orishas* born in heaven from *Olódumare*'s *ashé*.

iwereyeye: The rosary bead plant, *Abrus precatorius*.

jutía: An African bush rat, a large rodent; it is a staple offering for *orishas* such as *Elegguá, Ogún,* and *Ochosi*.

Lucumí: The word *Lucumí* is a contraction of various *Yoruba* words and translates as "my friend." As a people, the Lucumí are the physical, and now spiritual, descendants of the Yoruba slaves in Cuba. The word itself also refers to language that is now used in *Santería*.

maja: A nonpoisonous snake found in Cuba.

Marunlá: One of the sixteen *parent odu* in the *diloggún;* it is said to be opened when fifteen mouths fall face-up on the diviner's mat.

Merindilogún: One of the sixteen *parent odu* in the *diloggún;* it consists of sixteen open mouths and no closed mouths on the diviner's mat.

Merinlá: One of the sixteen *parent odu* in the *diloggún;* it is said to be opened when fourteen mouths fall face-up on the diviner's mat.

Metanlá: One of the sixteen *parent odu* in the *diloggún;* it is said to be opened when thirteen mouths fall face-up on the diviner's mat.

Mofá: The name of a mythological diviner found in the *patakís* of *odu*. The name is a contraction of "Moforibale Ifá! [I pay homage to Ifá!]."

mona: Spanish, a female monkey.

monita: Spanish, a young female monkey.

monito: Spanish, a young male monkey.

mono: The Spanish word for "monkey."

Obara: One of the sixteen *parent odu* of the *diloggún;* it is opened when six mouths fall face-up on the diviner's mat.

Obara Irosun: One of the sixteen *composite odu* found in the family of *Obara;* it forms when a casting of six mouths (*Obara*) is followed by a casting of four mouths (*Irosun*).

Obara Odí: One of the sixteen *composite odu* found in the family of *Obara*. It forms when a casting of six mouths (*Obara*) is followed by a casting of seven mouths (*Odí*).

Obatalá: An *orisha* considered to be king of all the *orishas* and the creator of humans.

obo: The Lucumí term for "monkey."

Oché: One of the sixteen *parent odu* in the *diloggún*. It is opened when five mouths fall face-up on the diviner's mat.

Oché Ejila: One of the sixteen *composite odu* that can fall in the family of *Oché*. It forms when a casting of five mouths (*Oché*) is followed by a casting of twelve mouths (*Ejila Shebora*).

Oché Ejioko: One of the sixteen *composite odu* that can fall in the family of *Oché*. It forms when a casting of five mouths (*Oché*) is followed by a casting of two mouths (*Eji Oko*).

Oché Irosun: One of the sixteen *composite odu* that can fall in the family of *Oché*. It forms when a casting of five mouths (*Oché*) is followed by a casting of four mouths (*Irosun*).

Oché Meji: One of the sixteen *composite odu* that can fall in the family of *Oché*. It forms when a casting of five mouths (*Oché*) is followed by another casting of five mouths.

Odí: One of the sixteen *parent odu* of the *diloggún;* it is opened when seven mouths fall face-up on the diviner's mat.

Odí Meji: One of the sixteen *composite odu* of the *diloggún;* it opens when a cast of seven mouths (*Odí*) repeats itself.

Odí Obara: One of the sixteen *composite odu* that can fall in the family of *Odí*. It forms when a casting of seven mouths (*Odí*) is followed by a casting of six mouths (*Obara*).

Odí Ogundá: One of the sixteen *composite odu* that can fall in the family of *Odí*. It forms when a casting of seven mouths (*Odí*) is followed by a casting of three mouths (*Ogundá*).

odu: The many patterns, or letters, that can fall when using the divination system known as the *diloggún*. There are a total of sixteen *parent odu* and 256 *composite odu*. Each of these has its own proverbs, *patakís,* meanings, and *ebós*. The word *odu* is both singular and plural in *Lucumí* and *Yoruba* usage.

Odúduwa: The founder of the *Yoruba* empire. He is also an *orisha*.

ofo: Loss.

Ofún: One of the sixteen *parent odu* of the *diloggún;* it is opened when ten mouths fall on the diviner's mat.

Ofún Irosun: One of the sixteen *composite odu* found in the family of *Ofún*. It opens when the initial cast of ten mouths (*Ofún*) precedes a cast of four mouths (*Irosun*).

Ofún Oché: One of the sixteen *composite odu* found in the family of *Ofún*. It opens when the initial cast of ten mouths (*Ofún*) precedes a cast of five mouths (*Oché*).

Ofún Ogundá: One of the sixteen *composite odu* found in the family of *Ofún*. This letter is open when the initial cast of ten mouths (*Ofún*) is followed by a cast of three mouths (*Ogundá).*

ogo: A witch, a sorcerer, or witchcraft.

Ogún: An *orisha* who is the patron of ironworkers and civilization.

Ogundá: One of the sixteen *parent odu* in the *diloggún;* it is opened when three mouths fall on the diviner's mat.

Ogundá Irosun: One of the sixteen *composite odu* in the family of *Ogundá*. It falls when a casting of three mouths (*Ogundá*) is followed by a casting of four mouths (*Irosun*).

Ogundá Meji: One of the sixteen *composite odu* found in the family of

Ogunda. It falls when a casting of three mouths (*Ogundá*) repeats itself.

Ogundá Obara: One of the sixteen *composite odu* found in the family of *Ogundá*. It falls when a casting of three mouths (*Ogundá*) is followed by a casting of six mouths (*Obara*).

Ogundá Unle: One of the sixteen *composite odu* in the family of *Ogundá*. It falls when a casting of three mouths (*Ogundá*) is followed by a casting of eight mouths (*Unle*).

Okana: One of the sixteen *parent odu* in the *diloggún;* it is opened when one mouth falls on the diviner's mat.

Okana Ejioko: One of the sixteen *composite odu* in the family of *Okana.* It falls when a casting of one mouth (*Okana*) is followed by a casting of two mouths (*Eji Oko*).

Okana Odí: One of the sixteen *composite odu* in the family of *Okana.* It falls when a casting of one mouth (*Okana*) is followed by a casting of seven mouths (*Odí*).

Okana Ejila: One of the sixteen composite odu in the family of *Okana.* It falls when a casting of one mouth (*Okana*) is followed by a casting of seven mouths (*Odí*).

Okana Meji: One of the sixteen *composite odu* in the family of *Okana.* It falls when a casting of one mouth, *Okana,* repeats itself.

Okana Ogundá: One of the sixteen composite odu in the family of *Okana.* It opens when a casting of one mouth (*Okana*) is followed by a casting of three mouths (*Ogundá*).

Olódumare: A *Yoruba* contraction that translates into "owner of the womb"; this is the supreme deity of the *Yoruba* and *Lucumí.*

Olófin: It is said among the *Lucumí* that Olófin is "god on earth"; he is the eldest avatar of *Obatalá* and can be received only by the priesthood of *Orúnmila,* the babalawos.

Olokun: The androgynous *orisha* who rules and owns the deepest parts of the sea.

olorí: The spirit enlivening the head; it was born in the *odu Ogundá Meji*.

omiero: Any number of herbal waters made by *Lucumí* priests.

ona: Afflictions.

òpèlè: The divining chain used by babalawos to access the 256 odu. The òpèlè is to the babalawo what the *diloggún* is to the santero.

oran: Moral and legal crimes.

orí: Refers to the part of one's spiritual consciousness remaining in heaven; it is a part of every person but never manifests on earth. As such, it is regarded as an *orisha,* and it may be received like any other *orisha*.

orisha: A *Yoruba* contraction that means "select head"; it denotes any of the myriad spirits in the pantheon of *Santería* that are an extension of Olódumare's *ashé*.

orún: Heaven; the invisible world. It is also a *Lucumí* word for "sun."

Orúnmila: The *orisha* worshipped by babalawos. Only men are called to his priesthood. He does not speak directly through the *diloggún;* however, certain composite odu indicate that he would like the one at the mat sent to his priests so that he may speak with him. He is also known as Orúnla.

Osá: One of the sixteen *parent odu* of the *diloggún;* it is opened when nine mouths fall on the diviner's mat.

Osain: One of the most mysterious *orishas*. Osain was created after creation; he sprang forth from the earth the moment the first green thing began to grow. He is the lord of *ashé* on the earth, knowing all herbal secrets. Without Osain, none of the *orishas* can work its magic, nor can its children be initiated, nor can the *orishas* be born on earth. He will live until the last green thing on this planet perishes. Anyone born with either six fingers or six toes is said to be his child by birth.

Osá Meji: One of the sixteen *composite odu* existing within the family of *Osá*. It forms when nine mouths (*Osá*) repeats itself, creating a twin.

Osá Ofún: One of the sixteen *composite odu* found in the family of *Osá*. It forms when a cast of nine mouths (*Osá*) precedes a cast of ten mouths (*Ofún*).

Osá Ogundá: One of the sixteen *composite odu* found in the family of *Osá*. It forms when the initial cast of nine mouths (*Osá*) precedes a cast of three mouths (*Ogundá*).

Osá Owani: One of the sixteen *composite odu* found in the family of *Osá*. It forms when a casting of nine mouths (*Osá*) precedes a cast of eleven mouths (*Owani*).

Oshún: The *orisha* bringing love, sweetness, money, prosperity, fertility, conception, and all the things that make life worth living to humans. She is sister to *Yemayá* and one of Shangó's three wives. She is also referred to as the "mother of twins."

osogbo: Negative influence; any of the evils that may be predicted for a client through the oracle known as the *diloggún*.

Owani: One of the sixteen *parent odu* of the *diloggún*; it is opened when eleven mouths fall on the mat.

Owani Meji: One of the sixteen *composite odu* in the family of *Owani*. It opens when the initial cast of eleven mouths (*Owani*) repeats itself, becoming a twin.

Owani Ogundá: One of the sixteen *composite odu* in the family of *Owani*. It opens when the initial cast of eleven mouths (*Owani*) precedes a cast of three mouths (*Ogundá*).

parent odu: The sign giving birth to all sixteen *composite odu* in a single family. For instance, *Okana* is a parent odu; it gives birth to the signs *Okana Ejioko, Okana Odí,* and *Okana Ejila*.

pataki: The many sacred stories and legends found in the *diloggún*; some of these are about the *orishas*, while others are about the actions of historical/mythological humans who lived and died in both Africa and Cuba. All *patakís* teach spiritual truths found in the *odu*.

perra: Spanish, a female dog.

perro: The Spanish word for "dog."

pollita: Spanish, a young female chicken.

rata: Spanish, a female rat.

rato: Spanish, a rat.

rogación: A cleansing of the head or *orí;* grated coconut is the main ingredient. It incorporates a series of prayers to strengthen and support the head. The specifics of each rogación are given in each *odu* of the *diloggún*.

Santería: The name of *orisha* worship as it developed in Cuba; the English translation from the Spanish is "worship of the saints." The name derives from the syncretizing of the Catholic saints and the *orishas* of the *Yoruba*.

speciesism: A term used by British psychologist Richard D. Ryder in 1973 to describe prejudice toward different species of animals and the random assignment of their value.

Unle: One of the sixteen *parent odu* found in the *diloggún*. It is formed when eight mouths fall on the mat.

Unle Ejioko: One of the sixteen *composite odu* found in the family of *Unle*. It is formed when a casting of eight mouths (*Unle*) is followed by a casting of two mouths (*Eji Oko*).

Unle Irosun: One of the sixteen *composite odu* found in the family of *Unle*. It is formed when a casting of eight mouths (*Unle*) is followed by a casting of four mouths (*Irosun*).

Unle Odí: One of the sixteen *composite odu* found in the family of *Unle*. It is formed when a casting of eight mouths (*Unle*) is followed by a casting of seven mouths (*Odí*).

Unle Ogundá: One of the sixteen *composite odu* found in the family of

Unle. It is formed when a casting of eight mouths (*Unle*) is followed by a casting of three mouths (*Ogundá*).

Unle Okana: One of the sixteen *composite odu* found in the family of *Unle*. It is formed when a casting of eight mouths (*Unle*) is followed by a casting of one mouth (*Okana*).

Yemayá: Born when *Olokun* was chained to the bottom of the ocean by *Obatalá*. Yemayá arose to become mother to the world and to the *orishas*. She is the patron of motherhood and of the fresh waters of the world.

Yemayá Asesu: One of the many avatars of *Yemayá*. She is known as the queen of ducks, geese, and swans. Her name means "the absent-minded one." She is closely associated with the *orisha Olokun*.

Yemayá Ibú Ogúnté Ogúnasomí: One of the many avatars of *Yemayá*. Some refer to her as *Yemayá Ibú Ogúnté,* or, simply, *Ogúnté*. In English, it means "Yemayá, the fierce one." She is closely associated with the *orisha Ogún*.

Yemayá Mayéléwo: One of the many avatars of *Yemayá*. She lives where the seven great tides of the ocean meet.

Yoruba: The native Africans, who originally settled in the southwestern parts of the area known today as Nigeria; their deities—the *orishas*—form the basis of the religion *Santería*. The word *Yoruba* also denotes the language shared by these peoples, the native tongue that mixed with Cuban Spanish to become *Lucumí*.

INDEX